D1518474

Çitlembik LTD.
Third Edition 2006
© Çitlembik Publications
© Orhan Yılmazkaya
© Photographs: Murat Oğurlu and Deniz Oğurlu

Library of Congress Cataloging–in–Publication Data

Yılmazkaya, Orhan
    Turkish bath , a light onto tradition and culture: a guide to the historic Turkish baths of İstanbul
    / Orhan Yılmazkaya; çev. Nancy F. Öztürk, Judith Ülgen; photographs Murat Oğurlu, Deniz
    Oğurlu.-3rd ed.-İstanbul: Çitlembik Yayınları,2006.
    144 p.: photo.
    Includes bibliographical references.
    ISBN: 975-6663-80-4
1.Baths, Turkish.-2.Public baths--Turkey-Istanbul.-3.Public baths--Turkey--Istanbul--Guidebooks
I.Title.II.Title:A guide to the historic Turkish baths of İstanbul

LC:RM821 2006
DC:725.73

Translated: Nancy F. Öztürk with Judith Ülgen
Publication editor: Murat Oğurlu
English editing: Carol LaMotte
Covers and layout: Deniz Akkol
Printing and binding: Mart Matbaası

Şeyh Bender Sokak 18/4 Asmalımescit Tünel 80050 İstanbul- TURKEY
Tel: +90 0212 292 30 32
252 31 63 Fax: +90 0212 293 34 66
www.citlembik.com.tr / kitap@citlembik.com.tr

A Light onto a Tradition and Culture

TURKISH BATHS

A Guide to the Historic Turkish Baths of Istanbul

Orhan Yılmazkaya
Photographs: Murat Oğurlu and Deniz Oğurlu
Translated by Nancy F. Öztürk with Judith Ülgen

Çitlembik

Contents

About this guide…

Turkish Baths: A Light onto a Tradition and Culture is the first book of its kind. It represents an attempt to cast a much-needed light onto a fascinating Turkish tradition and culture that is deeply rooted in the history of Anatolia.

Many tourists who visit Turkey are curious about the history, architecture and culture of the bath and many express an interest in going to a bath. Some are hesitant, though, as they do not know what they will meet there and what is expected of them. Actually, many young Turks today experience this same kind of hesitancy, as most of them have also not had first hand Turkish bath experiences. And while there are a scant handful of academic works that have been written about the Turkish bath, none has been especially designed to meet the needs of the uninitiated. There has also been no prior resource available that provides a complete list of names, addresses and features of the more than fifty historic baths that are still operating in Istanbul.

This book is a readable jaunt through the historic Turkish bath, its history, its traditions, and its culture. It also provides information about the kinds of items used in the past and those used today, the kinds of services offered, what the bather can expect, and what is expected of the bather. Finally, the book gives a complete guide to 50 of the still operating 57 historic baths of Istanbul. The book is fun to read as it provides highly interesting anecdotal information as well. Which famous pascha worked as a royal back scrubber when he was a lad? What about sex in the baths? And what about those lusty poems written by male bathers

for those oh-so-sweet lads who scrubbed them in the private cubicles?

There are all kinds of new bathing facilities in Istanbul: hotel baths, pay-for-shower places, saunas and the like, but this book ignores these modern facilities. This is a book about, and a guide to, Turkish baths in Istanbul. It's a good read for those looking for the perfect bath and for those who want to understand what the Turkish bath tradition is all about.

We divided the guide into European and Asian sides, and Europe again into historic peninsula (Beyazıt) and downtown (Beyoğlu). Not only do we provide names, addresses and contact information for the baths in the guide, we also talk about their architectural features and whether they are among the recommended. In point of fact, we suggest that you peek into as many of these baths as you can, for actually each of the 50 baths we visited is extremely interesting. The ones that we recommend, however, passed our "cleanliness" and "friendly staff" tests for those readers who will stay to bathe.

We worked hard on this book, as a glance at the reference list in the back and the photos we took will attest. Our hope is that we will have sparked the interest of those who read this book, that when they come to Istanbul they will visit and then enjoy the bath experience. The Turkish bath is not a 5-minute shower; it is a ritual that not only deeply cleanses the body, but deeply relaxes the bather. It is the massage of a lifetime. It is the act of becoming squeaky clean in architectural settings that are so beautiful they are almost mystical. It is one of those "must do" experiences as we live our lives.

Bath Culture: Past and Present

Life on our planet first appeared within water and it was only after millions of years of evolving that life began to prosper on land as well. However, even after they began to live on land, life forms still could not make do without water. Humans, too, of course have always had to make sure they have had access to sources of water on which to subsist, hence our ancestors' choice of the water's edge upon which to found nearly all of their great civilizations.

The Turkish language is full of meaningful expressions related to water; the Turks may praise another's spirituality and say that he or she is "as holy as water" and philosophize about life with "everything begins and ends with water." They also might comfort someone by "sprinkling water on the soul." They say, "water will clean everything but shame from a blushing face." These sayings demonstrate the importance of water to the Turks and point to the enduring bond between life and language.

The Ortaköy Bath built by the master architect Sinan, after restoration.

One of the most important features of water is its ability to dissolve other substances, making it our most traditional and most important cleansing agent. Even today, the numerous "technically advanced" cleansing agents available to us do not suffice to make us feel clean unless they are accompanied by tried and true water.

Evidence of humankind's preoccupation with cleanliness has been uncovered at many archaeological sites and researchers have determined that even societies separated by huge geographical distances and very different cultural practices display similar traditions and religious rituals regarding hygiene. Many religions exhort their believers to be clean in body and dress before they go before God. Islam demands not that the clothes worn by its followers be new or fashionable, but that the wearer's body and the clothes worn on it be clean.

We do not know exactly when it was that humans began bathing indoors, but the earliest evidence of this practice is found in India and ancient Egypt, as well as the bathing areas in the palaces of ancient Aegean and Greek civilizations. A ruin found along the banks of the Tigris in Mesopotamia is believed to be a bath dating to 859-824 BC during the reign of Assyrian Emperor Salmanasar III. At the Resülayn dig near the Turkish-Syrian border researchers have uncovered special areas set aside for bathing within the houses of that settlement. These third century BC spaces contained large clay pots used for bathing and water storage. A Hittite bathing area dating to 1200 BC was also discovered at a site near Gaziantep in Anatolia.

While archaeologists have found bathing sites and equipment used by a variety of civilizations spanning a wide range of time, it was in Athens at a 5th century BC site that the first commonly used heated bathhouses with a continual source of hot water were found. These round enclosures supported by rectangular rooms along the sides were heated by stoves.

Roman Baths

Though significant strides in bath construction were taken in ancient Greece, it was the Romans who developed the culture of independent bath construction. The Romans heated their houses with a system that very much resembles the central heating we use today. It was this same innovative heating system that the Romans later began using in their baths. Although not entirely confirmed, it is believed that in the first century BC an architect named Sergius Orata became the first to use air heated in a central furnace to heat a bathhouse. In 33 BC there were 170 baths in Rome alone. The number of baths sharply increased in this area when the emperor lifted the fees charged for bathing.

The Roman Empire's earliest monumental baths date from the first century BC. By this time, the baths of the Romans had developed into freestanding buildings that represented the typical "Roman Baths" as we know them. As the empire spread, so did the culture of the Roman bath, with public baths and bathrooms built in private and royal residences in places as far-flung as England, North Africa, Anatolia and the Middle East. Evidence of a Roman bath used for many years during the Byzantine Era has been uncovered in Ankara. Archaeologists have also found bath ruins in ancient Epheseus, Miletos, Pergumum, Priene, Side, and Antakya, all cities in today's Turkey. The "Great Bath" found in Side measures 41x55 meters. When he captured Diyarbakır at the end of the 5th century AD, the Sassanid Emperor Kubad I was very impressed with the Roman bath he found there.

Plan of the Diocletianus Bath built in Rome on an eleven hectare site.

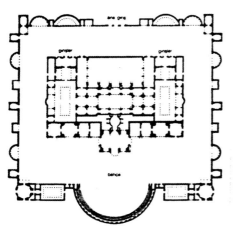

The Stabia Bath is Pompeii's earliest known public Roman bath. Following its construction in approximately 150 BC, the bath was enlarged with certain additions. Despite their considerable age, the plaster reliefs and frescos that decorate this bath have not lost their beauty. Much of the Caracalla Bath (205-217 AD) also remains standing today. This huge bath measures a full 220x114 meters. The bath complex even had its own library. The Diocletianus Bath (298-306 AD) with its gardens covered an eleven-hectare area. The bath was large enough to serve 3,200 persons simultaneously. Roman baths were generally very spacious facilities that were used for a number of activities not directly related to bathing: athletic performances, poetry readings, and games. These baths generally had large, portico-covered courtyards both at their fronts and backs where sporting events were held. Roman baths had large pools used commonly by all bathers. The bather first sat in the hot area and then took both hot and cold baths, followed by a massage and a deep scrub. The Romans decorated their baths with statues of their gods, military heroes, artists, and royalty. Small enclosures in the hot area of the bath were used to encourage profuse perspiration. Initially the Roman baths maintained separate bathing areas for men and women but later both sexes began to bathe in the same area and at the same time. This latter practice, though, was prohibited at the beginning of the 2nd century AD when the baths started to become a hub for prostitutes and their clients.

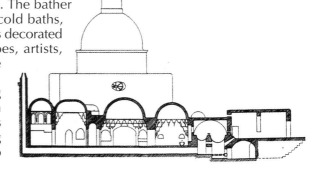

Cross-section of the Sinaniye Bath in Damascus.

The Romans had already bequeathed their bath traditions to the world when, by the beginning of the 5th century AD, their own baths began to lose their former architectural glory. The tradition of the bath did, however, continue to live on in the Eastern Roman Empire where it was passed down to the Byzantines. The construction of baths of both social and architectural importance thus continued during the Byzantine era.

With the fall of the Roman Empire, European practices of personal cleanliness were forced back to the home front. The grand pools of the magnificent Roman baths were replaced by the tradition of bathing in a small tub. Certain Christian authorities even disapproved of any kind of adult bathing and suggested that baths should not be taken more than once a month. In 11th century Spain, baths were viewed as the seat of evil and were blamed for the spread of syphilis. When the son of Spanish King Alphonso VI died in battle, the King decided that God was punishing him for frequenting baths, so he ordered that all public baths in his lands be destroyed. During the Middle Ages, it was commonly maintained by Spanish religious authorities that Moslems actually advanced the use of baths to wash away the sacred waters of Baptism. In fact, in the year 1568, following the expulsion of Moslems from Spain, the church ordered the destruction of all baths throughout the country, an order that caused an uprising among the people. Nevertheless, many of Europe's public baths were closed down during the 16th century. Thus it is recorded that in the following century, the French king, Louis 14th, washed only once a year, in the Spring, in contrast to their neighbors to the east, where bathing was so popular that certain western writers even claimed that Ottoman women had poor skin caused by washing too frequently.

In 120 AD, when the Roman Empire was still a monolithic power, Emperor Hadrian commissioned extensive infrastructure for the transport of water in Istanbul. A huge bath constructed in the same city by the Emperor Septimus could accommodate 2,000 bathers simultaneously. In a Byzantine document dating to 425-430, Istanbul—then Constantinople—is reported as having nine large and up to 150 small sized public baths, along with countless private baths located in palaces and homes. Unfortunately, none of the Roman or Byzantine

baths of Istanbul have survived to this date. The only remnants are sparse bath foundations adjacent to the Kalenderhane Mosque, which was converted from an earlier church, in the city's Şehzadebaşı neighborhood, and other foundations uncovered at the site of today's archaeological museum. Due to the lack of ruins, we have to glean our evidence about Istanbul baths of that period from writings of contemporary historians and from extant official documents.

Baths are the subject of some Istanbul legends that the Ottomans inherited from the Byzantines. One example is a legend claiming that Emperor Constantine I-- the first emperor of the Eastern Empire to accept Christianity and the emperor who gave his name to the city--began a flurry of construction during which he erected 27 sacred talismans intended to protect the city and its people. The eleventh talisman, described as a four-sided column made up of a thousand pieces is supposed to be buried under the Ottoman period Beyazit Bath. As the legend goes, the son of the sultan died suddenly of the plague when the column, which was supposed to ward off that disease, was knocked down during the construction of the stone bath, and that the plague then rapidly spread throughout the city. According to yet another story, the stones laid by a stonecutter who had prayed without first performing his ritual ablution would not stay in place and the job had to be finished by his apprentice.

Moslems, ordered by their religion to be clean in body and soul, were quick to inherit the tradition of the Roman bath. In the 8th century, the Islamic Uymayyids built their first baths in Syria. Today there is a small Umayyid bath in Israel that was built in 715. In architectural style it appears to be a direct continuation of the Roman bath tradition.

Within Syria, Lebanon, Jordan, Palestine, Israel, and Egypt--all countries that were once a part of the far-flung Roman Empire--there remain countless ruined and still erect baths built during various periods by Moslem governments. During the 14th century, there were 35-40 baths in Baghdad. A 20th century study listed sixty baths in the city of Damascus. One thing especially noteworthy about the baths of Damascus is that not one of the 60 baths is a double bath; that is, none was set aside for the sole use of women. It has been documented that in the 13th century there were 68 market baths in Aleppo. In the 17th century, the traveller Evliya Çelebi made note of 55 baths in Cairo. Another interesting point is that the Umayyids also built many baths in Spain during the 8th-15th centuries when they had political control of that region. Iran also has had numerous baths built during various Islamic regimes. During the 16th century, the Mongolian emperor Babur Shah also constructed large and magnificent baths in India.

The first baths to be built in Anatolia by a Moslem authority are believed to be the two Seljuk baths in the ancient Armenian city of Ani said to date from the second half of the 11th century. Another old bath is the Savurkapısı (Radviye) bath in the city of Mardin that was built one hundred years later by the Artuklu dynasty.

The Turkish Seljuks built baths across their Empire in Anatolia, with 13th century baths in Kayseri, Divriği, Kütahya, Ilgın, Kastamonu, Konya, Tokat, Beyşehir, and Alara. There are seven Seljuk Turkish baths in İzmir's Selçuk district alone. According to inscriptions, one of these baths was called the Saadet Hatun Bath. This bath reflects many of the characteristics of traditional Turkish baths. When compared to Roman baths, though, the Seljuk baths were both small and plain. The traditional Turkish style that was later to be repeated in Ottoman Turkish baths consists of a square plan with four arched side spaces and private cubicles at the corners, sometimes decorated with tilework.

Baths during the Ottoman Empire

The Anatolia Seljuk Empire expanded geographically by cutting huge swaths out of the Byzantine Empire. The much-weakened Byzantines finally disappeared altogether with the spread and final conquest of Istanbul by the Turkish Ottomans. The Ottomans built many of their finest architectural works in the capital city they had conquered. However, the Ottomans had already constructed some architectural wonders in their earlier capitals of Bursa and Edirne. In 1326, Murat I, the third Ottoman Emperor, captured Bursa where he restored the construction around an

Almost all paintings depicting Turkish baths are the works of western Orientalist painters.

earlier Byzantine hot spring and transformed it into a bath. Called the "Old-New (Eski-Yeni) Bath," this building still houses a functioning bath in Bursa.

Upon the conquest of Istanbul in 1453, Sultan Mehmet the Conqueror built nineteen baths in Istanbul, five of them quite large in size. The first Ottoman bath in the city was known as the Irgat Bath. In the 17th century, the famous traveler Evliya Çelebi wrote that this bath (unfortunately no longer standing) could accommodate five thousand bathers. In the same record, Çelebi also states that at that time İstanbul had 168 market baths. Evliya Çelebi made a list of each bath by name, remarking that their names gave the impression that each was set aside for people who lived or worked in a certain neighborhood. According to this classification, the ethnic or religious group designated for that particular bath could be easily understood. Some of the names are overly fanciful, however, and must reflect Çelebi's desire to entertain the reader.

An Ottoman–style miniature depicting a women's bath.

A list dating to 1886-87 gives the names and districts of 75 baths within the city walls. According to Mehmet Nermi Haskan in his recent and very useful book, İstanbul Hamamları (Istanbul Baths), a total of 237 baths were built in Istanbul; however, some of these are no longer traceable and the locations of some of those on record are unknown. One should keep in mind that only public baths were included in this list, small private baths built in the palaces and other grand residences having been excluded from the count as no information is available regarding these private baths.

The Ottomans not only built baths in the capital of Istanbul but also constructed countless baths across the wide sweep of their empire. Examples of Ottoman baths in various states of (dis)repair can be found in Europe, the Middle East and North Africa, with the westernmost Ottoman bath being that in the Hungarian city of Peçuy.

The Ottomans built thermal baths in those areas that had natural hot springs. While Turkish baths are based on the heating of cold water, thermal baths were built directly over hot springs. In contrast to the Ottoman bath type, these thermal baths had large, hot mineral water pools and it was commonly believed that these baths were curative for a number of diseases and ailments. The thermal baths, too, were a tradition inherited from the Romans, who also constructed their thermal baths over such natural hot springs.

In the Ottoman period, baths were often built as part of large religious charity complexes known as "külliye" that could include a mosque, hospital, soup kitchen, library, schools, and lodgings for students or clerics. In some cases, baths were also constructed as independent structures. Because the construction of these large charitable complexes would continue for many years, the bath was completed first so that laborers could bathe after working. The income from these baths, which were sponsored by foundations headed by the sultan, members of the royal family, or other leading figures in the Empire, would be used to maintain the mosque or other buildings in the complex. It has been documented that in the 16th century, empire officials used their personal wealth to build these charitable institutions. For example, Grand Vizier Rüstem Pasha had 32 baths built in various cities. Foundations established for other social purposes were often financed with the income from baths built in various city districts and cities throughout the empire. For hundreds of years, these baths drew in large and important sums of money that could be channeled to charity.

Private ownership of baths began in the second half of the 19th century. The baths established and owned by various charity foundations had, for hundreds of years, been managed by their own member committees, but eventually some unscrupulous individuals began funneling bath funds into their

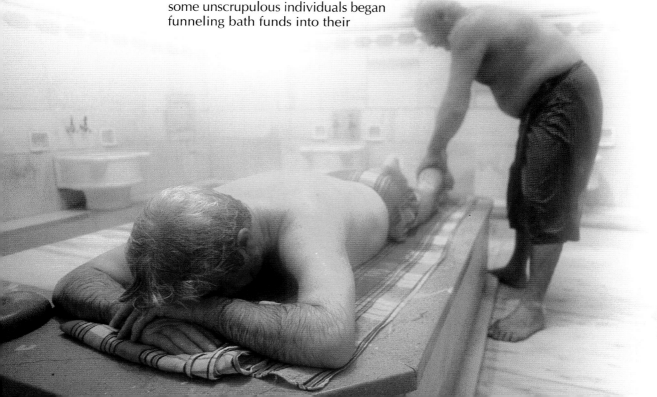

own pockets instead of passing them on to the charities as intended. This led to a drop in income for the baths and a consequent change in organization as the foundations began renting the baths out to private enterprisers. This, in turn, paved the way for private ownership of baths. Today, other than a scant handful of charity-owned baths, all the working baths of Istanbul are the deeded property of private individuals or companies. Even though the profitable income earned by some of the privately-owned baths has contributed to their preservation, for the most part, the transfer of baths from charity foundations to private hands has opened the way for the eventual decline of these institutions. Today, in addition to the bath buildings that have been abandoned and are gradually falling into a state of ruin, others are being used as depots, workshops, stores, and exhibition halls, while some are even functioning as public-access toilets. While the charities were meticulous record keepers when it came to the use and income of the baths, private proprietors have historically failed –and continue to fail- to keep any such records.

Even after the baths passed to private hands, however, at least some of the traditions common to the charity baths were continued, or at least the local and central authorities tried to ensure that some of the former practices were maintained. One of the best-known examples of this kind of continuation of tradition is free or discounted bathing for the poor, homeless, travelers and conscripts. An event recorded in 19th century Istanbul reflects the interesting changes that were taking place there at that time. The writer, Basiretçi Ali Efendi, said he plead with the municipal authorities to intervene as some of the bath attendants were curt with the soldiers, most likely because they bathed at a low charge, and that sometimes the soldiers were refused services by being told that there was no water that day or that the water was cold, or else were simply handed wet towels or wrapping cloths. The writer also supposed that nowhere else in the world would soldiers be treated so meanly and reiterated that the duties of any soldier were much more vital to the society than those of any bath attendant.

Some baths built during the Ottoman era to serve a specific institution or group of people were gradually transformed into public-access baths, a development most likely caused by neglect on the part of the sponsoring group. One example of such a case is the Acemoğlu Bath of Şehzadebaşı, which closed down only a few years ago. This bath was an extension of the Janissary barracks set aside for young recruits, known as the "Acemi Oğlanlar," hence the name of the bath. After the Janissaries were disbanded, the bath continued to function, but this time serving the public. Nearby is another bath, the Vezneciler Bath, which was first part of a private residence before it, too, was converted into a public bath.

Excessive water consumption was an inevitable consequence of the bath's

The wooden cupola (sky lantern) of the Tahtaminare Bath in Balat.

The hot section of the Hacı Kadın Bath of Kocamustafapaşa.

popularity during the Ottoman era. Those who wanted to build any facility that used water were required to first pay for the transport of this water supply to the city. Water from springs found outside of the city was transported in pipes leading to the central water supply. In the construction of a bath, the proprietor first had to comply with the law by augmenting city water supplies before he could construct his bath. At the time, the amount of water to be used was written on the deed in "masura" measurements. The bath then "owned" this amount of water which it therefore had the right to use free-of-charge. The ordinary bath required 1.5 to 2 masura of water daily, one masura equaling approximately 14.5 cubic meters. Baths that failed to acquire their own water supplies in the aforementioned manner often dug wells on the bath grounds. Such baths were then operated in accordance with the amount of water found in the well. This water management system continued on unimpeded until the 1980s when the city changed the laws on the books and began charging baths for water, going so far as to charge those baths operating on water being drawn from their own wells.

In the Ottoman period, wood was used for most heating purposes, but other fuel has been mentioned. In his travelogue, Evliya Çelebi reported that the baths of Diyarbakır and Arabia burned the city's garbage to heat their baths. According to another report, Sultan Abülhamit II (1879 – 1909), angered by the growing reform movement, burned these opposition publications in the pit of the Çemberlitaş Bath. He only desisted after word of this was leaked - and the new stokepit he had built in the State Printing House to replace it was completed.

Water and wood consumption was so high during the Ottoman period that the government was forced to pass conservation measures. An edict issued by the ruling sultan of the day in the 18th century forbade the construction of new baths. Despite the ban on construction, the consumption of wood eventually reached such proportions that the Great Çamlıca Forest was entirely destroyed after being sold as fuel to the proprietor of the Grand Bath of Üsküdar in the second half of the 19th century. Even today, most baths are heated with wood and wood shavings, while only a handful have switched to natural gas or fuel oil.

Islam and Baths

The effect of Islam on daily life during the Ottoman period led to many discussions regarding baths. One practice upon which Moslems agree is the "minor" ablution they are required to perform before doing their daily prayers or participating in other religious rites or ceremonies, the "full" or "gusül" ablution required after sexual relations, masturbation, menstruation or birth. Frequent bathing is also highly recommended to the faithful who wish to follow the Prophet's example.

From its courtyard, we can see that the original domes and chimney of the Süleymaniye Bath are still intact.

The Arabs, though, did not build baths for the use of women, nor did they send their women to the baths that did exist. According to those sects that forbade women from attending a bath, there were narratives whereby the Prophet is supposed to have said, "Let not he who believes in God and the Day of Judgment enter a bath without covering; and let not he who believes in God and the Day of Judgment send his women to a bath." They also base their belief on the narrative, "The woman who undresses in any place other than her husband's house, removes the covering between herself and God."

The majority of the Ottoman Empire's Moslem population, however, conformed to the beliefs of the Hanefi sect. According to Hanefi teaching, women are free to go to baths as long as they do not expose those areas of their bodies as proscribed by Islamic law, which states that both men and women should cover their "private parts," that is, the parts of their body extending from their knees to their waists. It is considered sinful to expose this area, except for those special circum stances under which it is permitted. When taking a bath, the bather uses a thin wrap called a "peshtamal" to conceal his or her private area. Having this private area seen or touched is also prohibited, meaning that it is sinful to have this area massaged or scrubbed by others. Massaging of the feet is considered to be demeaning to the scrubber and it is considered extremely rude for anyone to request this kind of service.

Despite all of the detailed regulations, or perhaps because of them, it was easier for Ottoman women to bathe than it was for men. The Ottomans governed their citizens of various religions and ethnic backgrounds on a foundation of "separate but equal." The proscriptions against non-Moslem men were also much more rigid than those against non-Moslem women. According to these regulations, Moslems and non-Moslems were prohibited from using the same items at the bath. For example, the peshtemals used by the Moslems were easily distinguished form those used by non-Moslems. Non-Moslems did not wear the wooden slippers into the bath and used separate dressing rooms and bathing cubicles.

Scrubber personnel had the right to refuse to wash a non-Moslem. It was expected that bath staff would ensure that these practices were carried out without unduly disturbing or offending the Moslem clientele. It was in practice, though, only in the very rarest of cases that non-Moslems were barred from attending any bath. During the Ottoman period Christians and Jews did not experience any problems entering a bath, but they did have to abide by the segregation restrictions imposed. To conform to Jewish practices, the baths in predominantly Jewish neighborhood had small pools, called "mikveh," into which the bather would enter. These pools had to contain a minimum of 720 liters of water and Jewish bathers entered them to cleanse their entire bodies when they washed before the Sabbath, as well as following menstruation and birthing. Upon request, these baths were used only after the water had been blessed by a rabbi.

During the Ottoman years there were many more baths than there are today and these baths played an important role in the everyday life of the Ottoman citizen. There were countless baths in Istanbul that were renowned for their large size, the purity of their water, their spaciousness, the skills of their men and women scrubbers and massagers, their relationship with sacred individuals, the belief that they were curative, and for the politeness and experience of the bath managers. Other than very rare exceptions, these "market" or "public" baths were open for all those who could afford to pay the small entrance fee.

The Bath: The Only Place a Woman Could Visit

Other than the relaxation seen in the later years of the Ottoman Empire (primarily affecting those in the upper and educated classes) urban Ottoman women lived their lives in an atmosphere of restriction and restraint, forced to spend their time in their homes or in quarters set aside for women only. No woman could leave her home unattended and it was considered highly unseemly for a woman to leave her home too frequently, even if attended. Her father, and later her husband, oversaw her every movement.

The bath was the one--and thereby of course very welcome--exception to these restrictions. Every week or two Ottoman women would arrange bath excursions with their female relatives, close friends, and neighbors. The bath was a kind of women's club, providing an important space in which the Ottoman women were free to carry out their social lives.

Contrary to male bath traditions, women attended the baths en masse. The preparations carried out before going to the bath were also a social activity in and of themselves, while they also reflected the social and economic class of the bath-goer. Parties held at the baths became important events. Certain

Part of the women's section of the Çemberlitaş Bath was torn down in the 19th century to widen a road.

occasions traditionally called for a bath as well, such as the "Bride's Bath," the bath to wash and compliment the new mother, the bath to again compliment the girl who has just become engaged, the bath of the young boy child who has just become circumcised, the "15th day bath," and the "soldier's bath."

For women of means, the list of items necessary for attending the bath was a long one. These grand ladies also required more attention at the bath, which meant that they had to hire more attendants; thereby increasing the amount of money they spent there. Thus a woman's bath allowance could represent a sizeable expense for her husband. Special bundles were prepared for the bath. These beautifully wrapped bundles would include embroidered silk peshtemals, raised sandals of wood, ivory, and/or silver to keep the feet out of water, pure white soap, henna, kohl, a mirror, comb and brush, an assortment of towels, loufa cloths, silver bath bowls for pouring water over the body, and a set of clean clothes. The steward of the house would carry the lady's bundle to the bath and then attendants would prepare her dressing room and bathing cubicle with all of her accroutrements. When these kinds of important personages were bathing, the bath would also prepare a post-bath refreshment for the lady to enjoy. This refreshment could either be a jug of boza, a traditional beverage made of fermented millet, or a variety of pickles, depending on the district. Meanwhile, women vendors on hand in an area near the dressing rooms stood ready to sell and serve homemade sesame sweets.

Fausto Zonaro's Painting, "Welcome"

Actually a tradition that the Turks inherited from the Byzantines, the "Bride's Bath" was an important social event. Held on a Tuesday, two days prior to the actual marriage, the bath party would be organized by the bride's family who would invite every female relative possible from their own and the groom's family. As part of the Bride's Bath ceremony, the bride-to-be, dressed in her finest, would greet each guest as they entered the bath. The guests would then be served a large assortment of refreshments before moving into the first "warm" area of the path. There the bride's head would be covered with a large veil and then she would be led around the room and finally into the hot bath area, followed in a procession by all the guests. Here the guests would sing, make speeches complimenting the bride, dance, and pray while they and the bride were washing. Once she was washed, the bride was led amongst the guests three times. Family members took turns pouring water over her head, using either gold or silver urns according to the social standing of the family. They would then toss coins over her head and onto the main hot stone in the center of the bath. They would also toss cumin seeds at the bride, and her finger- and toenails would be tinted with henna. As the coins fell from her head to the floor, they would be scooped up by young unmarried girls who believed that they brought good luck. Gifts were presented to the bride while bath attendants and female musicians also received extravagant tips. The tradition of the Bride's Bath continues, in part, even today.

Fifteen days after the consummation of the marriage, the new wife would be brought back to the bath and yet another bathing party--the 15th day bath--would ensue. Should the wife conceive after the marriage, another celebratory bath as socially important as the bride's bath, the "postpartum" or "forty day" bath, would follow. According to popular belief that continues even to this day, babies should not be taken outside of the home for the first forty days of their lives. Furthermore, the baby should not come in contact with another baby under the age of 40 days or with a woman, other than its mother, who has recently given birth, otherwise the baby will be weak. In the Ottoman period, the "40 day bath" represented the baby's first excursion from the home. The staff at the bath were warned beforehand that such a baby would be in attendance and they were to ensure that no other baby or new mother would be present. A large group would accompany the baby to the bath as it celebrated its fortieth day of life. In the bath ceremony, the mother and baby would be washed by the mother's midwife. After washing the mother, the midwife would wrap a wide scarf around the mother's waist. The midwife would then dip her hand forty times into a vessel of water before slowly pouring this "forty times water" over the mother's head and letting it run over her body. The midwife would next wash the baby. A duck egg that had been beaten into a froth in a small pot would be smeared over the baby's body. The midwife would then dip a golden coin into the flowing water as she thrice repeated the Islamic prayer, the Fatiha.

Jean-Dominque Ingres, "Turkish Bath" 1862.

The baths were also perfect places for prospective mothers-in-law to find suitable brides for their sons. While the men at any Turkish bath were (and still are) careful to conceal their privates under their tightly wrapped peshtemals -- after all there were, and still are, signs all over the baths warning them to do so--such modesty was not so evident on the women's side. This meant that a mother could get a good look at the bodies of the young girls in their set and then choose the prettiest and healthiest looking girl as a potential daughter-in-law. Another tradition connected to the women's bath was the cleansing of a former prostitute. It was generally held that any prostitute who decided to forgo the life could be entirely cleansed with a special "forty times over" bath that would cleanse her of the "filth" of her profession. According to this very ancient tradition, the bather would first do three ritual ablutions. The bath attendant would then toss the woman's gold ring or earring into a jug of water and count to forty before pouring the water over the woman. The attendant then prayed and wished aloud for the woman's cleanliness of body and soul as she washed her thoroughly. The former prostitute thus became a "former" prostitute as she had been entirely cleansed of her former life.

The soldier bath party is organized by the young man's mother a week or two after he leaves for the service. Close relatives and neighbors are invited to this bath. Refreshments and entertainment are provided at this bath as well; all expenses being paid for by the mother. As they pour water over their bodies, the guests wish that the young man "should go and come as swiftly as water."

Jean Etienne Liotard, "Frankish Woman and Servant at the Turkish Bath" 1743

Derived from this is the still popular tradition of pouring water behind a loved one upon his or her departure.

Almost all baths have a "saint's basin" where women bathers will pray or make their wishes. In order to make their wishes come true, the petitioner will pay for another's bath or else donate a broom, wooden slippers, soap or shampoo to the bath.

Some still believe that the saint, Merkez Efendi, comes at night to bathe at the Merkez Efendi Bath in Topkapı. Until very recently, petitioners who left towels and peshtemals in the cubicle would claim that they were wet the next morning when they came back to retrieve them. There is also a belief that those who have died to uphold the faith come here to bathe.

It is also a very old belief in both Ottoman and Turkish cultures that baths are springs of health. This is especially true for those baths that are located near the graves of a holy individual. People would come to the Süleymaniye Bath because they believed that bathing here would cure hepatitis. Those who came to the bath for this purpose would drop a small piece of metal, like a steel needle for instance, into a water jug above which someone who was a "powerful breather" (someone who could pray with deep conviction) had prayed. They would then wait for the metal to turn yellow. If the metal object turned yellow, it was believed that the hepatitis had passed from the ill person to the water and that the disease would be cured. The patient would then swallow a drop of this water and then pour the rest over his or her head while praying.

Baths have played a much more meaningful role in the social lives of women than those of men. One more example to prove this point is that in the past--and still sometimes today--a woman might ask a bath attendant to collect some dirty bath water for her. She will then use this water for whatever magic spell she--or a person apt at this kind of thing--is drumming up. These women will insist that the water given to them has been defiled in one way or another. Some will come to the bath in the early morning hours requesting any water left standing in a kurna, one of the water basins. Most bath attendants will not comply with this kind of request, for the attendants have their own superstition: bathwater must never leave the bath. This superstition is based on the belief that the dirty water will be used for a spell that will bring misfortune to its victim.

Abdullah Buhari, "Washing Woman," 1741-1742

Another belief is that djinns come to the baths at night. Djinns are supposed to live in dirty places so bathhouses make perfect djinn houses. The djinns play all sorts of tricks on people. They might fool a young girl, often by tricking her into believing she is being invited to a "bride's bath" and then once the poor girl is there alone with the djinn they might compromise her honor. The djinns aren't just up to naughty tricks though. They may also take the form of fairies who will promise poor women that they will give birth to girls "whose smiles will cause roses to bloom and whose tears will turn into pearls." If those with a humpback manage to fall asleep at the bath at night, they might very well meet up with djinns who will start singing. The humpback and the djinns will then dance and the twisted spine will magically straighten.

While baths used to be an essential part of women's social life, their importance has dwindled in the last century, as Turks of all economic levels have begun installing indoor bathing facilities. This has caused both the total number of working baths to drop sharply, as well as a decrease in the number of customers who attend those baths that have managed to remain open. Other than the handful of baths that attract tourists, the average bath proprietor faces severe economic constraints and has to struggle just to keep his doors open. According to data released by the municipality, in 1943 there were 85 baths operating in Istanbul, all of them housed in historical structures. These baths attracted an average of 200 customers each day. Some of these baths had special

*Dowries of the rich were
sure to include a silver bath
pouring bowl.*

arrangements with the city such that the poor could bathe there for free.

Today there are 57 working historical baths in Istanbul, and their clientele is well under 200 per day. One new change, however, has been the number of new small baths and saunas built on the ground or lower levels of the high-rise buildings that are mushrooming all over the city. No one can provide the exact numbers of these kinds of establishments, but their architectural styles, kinds of operations, heating systems, and modus operandi are very different from that of the traditional Turkish bath. All five-star hotels in Turkey have their own "Turkish baths." However, although they may appear similar to the Turkish bath, be aware that they do not provide the same kind of atmosphere and services as the original baths.

In May 2002, news agencies picked up a story that was widely published across Turkey. According to the story, the economic crisis had forced four different historical baths in the town of İnegül in Bursa to close their doors to women, thus ending a tradition of women's day baths that had continued unimpeded there for 540 years. The four proprietors reported that their number of clientele had dropped through the years, restricting their incomes. Then when the economic crisis hit, the owners found themselves unable to cover the high costs of the water consumed by their women customers who, unlike the males, would spend the whole day at the bath with their friends and relatives. The owners said that the women consumed more water in a single day than the male clientele consumed in an entire week. They said they could no longer meet this expense and were therefore forced to close the women's side of the bath.

Very few of these authentic soap boxes can be found today.

During the time of the Ottoman Empire, there were a few traditions when men also attended the baths as a group. The most famous example of such was the baths taken by the fire squads after they had extinguished a fire. If the fire was extinguished during the day, the fire fighters simply attended any bath as an individual customer, but if the fire was extinguished at night, the entire crew would go all together to a bath reserved just for them. Because these fire squads were considered government employees, they would not be charged for bathing. During the fasting month of Ramadan, the largest baths would traditionally organize an iftar (the meal that "breaks the Ramadan fast") for the leaders of the fire brigades. Men also had a few traditional group baths, among them the bath for the groom and the circumcision baths. In the latter tradition, the boy to be circumcised was taken to the bath the day prior to his circumcision. He would be washed and then the palms of his hands stained by a tiny spot of henna. The Armenian grooms had their group baths with their own special customs as well. For example, the Armenians would break an egg over the head of the prospective groom and then all the young men at the bath would have a grand egg fight. This tradition represented a way for men to wish the soon-to-be married young men a life of fertility.

The beautiful inlaid wooden clogs of the past have been replaced by crude wood-soled or plastic slippers.

Although in smaller groups than those of the women, Ottoman men might also attend the bath with a group of friends who would use this opportunity to converse as they reclined together on the central heating stone. A verse written in the 19th century by poet Aşık (Bard) Rüzi reflects the atmosphere of just such a bathing experience: "The boy bath attendant is pretty, so pretty; rose water sherbet to balm ardent spirits; The talk at the center stone is lively, so lively; When joined by the barber so beautiful, beautiful."

There was a special kind of bath that served the homeless or those who were too drunk to make it home. These were the "all night" baths. Today this writer could find only one remaining bath of this kind. It, like its forerunners, serves as a kind of hotel that at midnight begins accepting men who will spend the night.

An old tradition that still continues is that of keeping the baths open all night on Thursdays. Friday is the holy day of the week for Moslems and the night prior is considered to be time of preparation. The baths are kept open on that night to meet the bathing needs of all the worshipers who will attend Friday prayer the next day.

Bath culture has become so intertwined with Turkish culture as a whole that many sayings related to baths and bathing have entered the Turkish language. There is also a whole body of slang related to baths, some having to do with the goings-on in the women's baths and some with the homosexual relations that occurred on both sides of the building.

The bath is traditionally a hotbed of gossip, a place where women may find themselves getting into arguments or even fights. Hence the term "Shrew's Bath" for any chaotic situation in which everyone is talking at the same time and nobody is listening to the other. Up until a few years ago, there were bear handlers who would walk through the streets offering entertainment. Upon the payment of a small fee, the handler would have his bear do tricks. One was to have the bear lie on his back and swing his four legs into the air. This was called the "old lady faints at the bath" trick. Mothers would bring their children with them to the bath. When a boy got of a "certain age," other customers might complain that he was too old to be bathing with them. The bath attendant would warn the mother by chiding, "Madam, the next time you should also bring your husband." A "Bath Mama" signified an obese woman or one that was cruel at heart. "Saving the bath's morals" was a metaphor for someone who was trying to explain away a wrongdoing. A really hot environment was "like a bathhouse." "He who goes to the bath must sweat" refers to the inevitable difficulties inherent in some tasks. Despite the fact that today's bath proprietors find themselves in severe financial straits, Turks still use the expression of "owner of a brand-new bath" to describe someone who is incredibly rich in property. People who tend to be extremely boastful are described as "bath singers." The person who cannot keep a secret is said to be somebody who "echoes every sound like a bath heating stone." The importance of properly hosting a guest is emphasized by "you can't treat a guest with bath water." People who are easy to please are described as being the kind of people "who fall in love with the piper at the wedding, and with the water basin at the bath." Their difficult opposites become then those "who don't like the music at the wedding, nor the basin at the bath."

The person who "becomes friends with the bath water" is the kind who chooses the wrong sort of people for friends. Those situations that never seem to change are "old jugs and old baths." When a mystic is "taken to the bath" in the world of Mevlana dervish mystics, it means the person has completed all of the required initiation trials and is thus ready to be taken to the bath where he will finally be able to remove the clothes worn during the long trial, bathe, and put on new clothes before having the honor of sitting on the fur mat.

A "bath boy" is slang for a homosexual. "Bath money" is both the money paid to the "boy" for his fee, or is used to describe a sum of money given to someone to insult or humiliate. A "bath goer" is someone who is canonically unclean. The "bath clubs" are teams or other groups who are mocked as weak, unimportant, or considered generally worthless. Students talk about having to go to the "bath" if they are going to be called before a disciplinary committee, as they will be made to perspire once they get there.

Ottoman Turkish baths often crop up in literary works, too. There was even a type of classical Ottoman "Divan" poetry termed, "Hammamiye," i.e., poems devoted to public baths. The single poem variety--the Hammamname (letter pertaining to the bath)--was used to describe a particular bath's architecture, to compliment a bath attendant, or to describe the conversations or various sorts of entertainment that took place there. Most of these poems are in the format of the classical kaside, a commemorative poem consisting of more than 15 rhyming couplets. Written in the 16th century, the earliest of these bath poems sometimes describe the love relations experienced in the baths. Folk literature also has examples of epics that describe baths. At the beginning of the 19th century, Tosyalı Aşık (Troubadour) Mustafa Divan came to Istanbul where he proceeded to write a 150-strophe epic in praise of the baths he saw here. In addition, baths are also topics and scenes in Turkish theater, folk theater, and puppet plays.

Baths use and used a large variety of bath-specific items, some of which are no longer being produced and many of which are becoming more and more difficult to locate. Among the more beautiful bath accessories are the small, hand-worked brass, silver, or copper basins and the beautifully worked clogs. The basins are actually small shallow bowls used for dipping the clean water from the stone kurna (a kind of sink that is only used to collect clean water and which is never polluted in any way). The bather, sitting on a small stool near the kurna, pours the clean water over her body or has it poured for her by an attendant or friend. In some parts of Turkey still today, the dowry of a girl from a well-to-do family will include a silver bath basin. Even though the bath provided such basins for their customers, Ottoman upper-class women always took their own basins with them. This wonderful tradition is fast falling out of favor. The bath owners complain that when the metal basin comes in contact with the marble kurna it makes a grating sound and that is why they today substitute plastic basin bowls for the copper or silver examples of yore.

The kinds and quality of items a woman brought with her to the bath represented the bather's social status and class. One of such indicators was the nalın--the special raised clog women wore on their feet in the baths. These kept the feet out of any water and were also believed to protect the wearer from any annoying antics of the djinns. The five-inch clogs were made of wood to prevent slipping. The upper parts of the nalın were covered with mother of pearl, tortoise shell or silver repoussé. The nalın used by new brides, mothers, or women of rank were traditionally covered with worked silver. These nalın were never taken home but were rather left in the care of the bath attendant. Unfortunately, the craft of nalın-making has disappeared. In their place, today bathers either used very plain and unadorned wooden clogs called takunya or machine-stamped plastic slippers.

Another bath item that is no longer used today is the box used for carrying soap. The box was large enough to hold a large bar of soap and had tiny holes punched in the bottom that permitted the soap to drain and dry. Made of copper, steel or silver, these special soap holders are today found only in antique shops.

Among the other bath accessories were the body scrubbing cloths made of woven date root fibers, the embroidered towels and peshtamals woven in the Ottoman textile center of Bursa, a special powder used to remove unwanted body hair, and pumice stones for foot and knee care.

The Turkish Bath through European Eyes

By the 18th century, the Ottoman bath began drawing the attention of Europeans

who started to emulate the Turks by constructing similar baths in their own countries. The source of this interest was undoubtedly the accounts of the European travelers who had started to flock to the "exotic orient" together with the tradesmen and diplomats who traveled there on business. In their correspondence and articles, Europeans--who had long before forgotten the tradition of the grand Roman baths--began referring to these kinds of baths as "Turkish baths."

We derive our most detailed historical information about Ottoman baths from reports written by Luigi Bassono. Assigned as an envoy to the Topkapı Palace in the first half of the 16th century, Bassono's work, printed in Rome in 1545, includes mention of baths he had visited in various regions of the Empire. Bassono gave detailed information about one of these baths and said that it reminded him very much of a bath he had seen in Rome. Bassono also mentioned the fact that customers could use as much water as they wished (a feature that continues to this day) and that bathers never fully exposed themselves while bathing.

Continuing with Bassano's account, he said that middle and lower class women would go to the bath, usually their neighborhood bath, in groups of up to twenty women. There were some instances, rare as they might be, where women would go to a more distant bath that was considered to be more luxurious. Bassano claimed that the tradition of women washing each other at the bath sometimes led to more intimate relations. He said that because the baths represented their only opportunity to leave the confines of their homes, it was a popular activity and that they would stay at the baths from morning to early evening. The Italian traveler also related that women of means had two male servants carry their bath items to the bath, among the items that would be taken were bundles of clean clothes, food baskets, pillows, and kilims. He also wrote that the trip to the bath meant a great deal of fun for women of all classes.

In a book he had published in Paris in 1553, Pierre Belon wrote that Turks had to be the cleanest people living on this earth and that they far-surpassed Europeans in terms of childcare, nutrition, and cleanliness. He added that the baths of Istanbul played a positive role in the general well-being of the population.

Writing in 1608, a German traveler originating from Nürnberg named Schweigger penned his own observations about the Ottoman baths. Schweigger described how the bath attendant would massage and deep scrub the bather and then clean the feet with pumice stones. He complained though of the pain associated with the bloodletting used to cure various ailments. Scheigger also described how the baths prepared a special depilatory cream and how this was used to remove unwanted body hair. The white cream of a mud consistency made from a mixture of lime and arsenic water was smeared on the dry body. After waiting five or six minutes the unwanted hair could be wiped away. This cream used to be found at all baths but now it is available at only a couple of baths. Schweigger reported that the cream immediately removed hair but if left on too long could damage the skin. Sometimes the depilatory caused a burning sensation and so soothing creams were used on the body after its use.

Another traveler to write down his impressions of the Ottoman baths was Baron Wenceslav Vratislav, a member of a group sent by Rudolf II, emperor of the Roman German Empire, to visit the Ottoman Empire in 1597. Vratislav was quite young when he first arrived in the Empire and he spent two of his three years on Ottoman soil as a hostage. In addition to his descriptions of the baths, he also wrote of his impressions of other cultural and social aspects of the Ottomans. He described the hot water spring baths and related the case of an Istanbul bath manager who was punished for not having provided a customer with a towel. According to his account, the local judge, the kadı, punished the hapless man with a thousand canes, stipulating that he would be caned two hundred times on his buttocks, two hundred on the soles of his feet, two hundred on the calves,

La Barbier, "Turkish Bath," a copper plate print technique.

and three hundred on the abdomen. He said that after this caning the man "was as swollen as a baby pigeon chick emerging from the egg" and added that it was difficult to ascertain if he was a man or a kind of monster. Baron Vratislav wrote that married Ottoman women were frequent visitors to the baths and that, before marriage, some women forced their prospective husbands to promise not to interfere with their attendance. He said that women based this freedom to bathe on some of the sacred sayings.

In addition to these accounts by male travelers, three western women who traveled to Istanbul in the 18th and 19th centuries also wrote down their reactions to Ottoman baths. Each woman had a lively account of her bath experience. Mrs. Harvey, an English woman who was the author of a book called Travels, was not particularly impressed with the Ottoman bath. "At one point I felt like a steamed lobster. Animals can feel when they are being boiled and I felt too that I was being boiled alive…When I looked at my friend, I saw that her face was as red as a beet. Close to fainting, we pleaded that they "get us out of here." But our pleading was all in vain. We were boiled and sanded down and boiled again and sanded down, just as the tradition demanded…."

Some Englishmen who had had come to the Ottoman Empire for diplomatic reasons in the 19th century decided to build baths in England once they returned home and it was at this time that the Handbook of Turkish Baths was published. These baths had sub-floor heating and were built first in England and then in Germany where they were called Roman-Irish baths.

Because most Ottomans believed the painting of pictures to be forbidden by Islam, the only paintings we have of Ottoman baths are those done by western artists. Found today in western libraries and museums, some of these paintings were painted by those who actually did travel to the Ottoman Empire, while others are entirely figments of the imagination, dreamed up by artists who had never actually traveled to Turkey.

An Austrian architect named Heinrich Glück traveled to Istanbul during the First World War and spent much of his time studying baths. He studied dozens of baths, photographing many of them, and even drawing the plans of twenty-two different examples. All of this data was collected into a work called Die Bader Konstantinopels that was published in Vienna in 1921.

In his book, Gurbet Hikayeleri (Migrant Tales), Turkey's famous novelist and journalist Refik Halit Karay, who lived during the transition from the Ottoman Empire to the Turkish Republic, described the bath in his childhood home. According to Karay, the family bathed once every ten days and it took the bath one to two days to heat up and then four to five days to cool down again. On bath day the whole family would take turns bathing, the women during the day and the men in the evening.

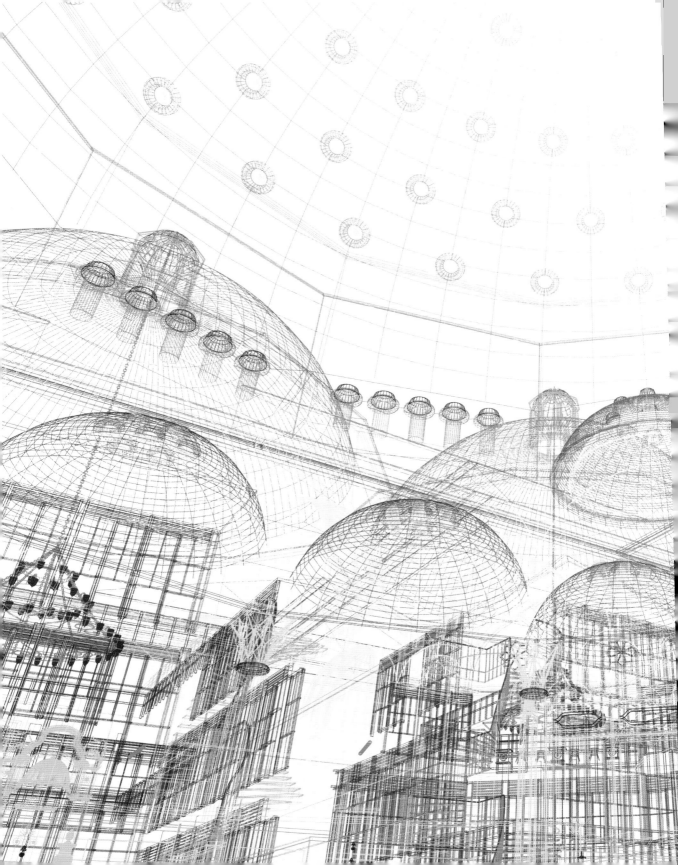

Ottoman Bath Architecture:
Warmth and Light under the Central Dome

Ruins of a Roman-era bath uncovered in Epheseus present researchers with a valuable opportunity to trace the development of the bath from the Roman to the Ottoman Turkish type. The heating system is the essential key to understanding just how the baths developed architecturally.

The hot areas of both Roman and Ottoman types were built over a brick platform. Adjacent to this hot area was the külhan, the stokepit or the fire pit used to heat the baths and the water used. The heat and smoke from this pit was carried below the floors via conduits termed "hellish paths." After heating the rooms and the water, the heat was expelled from the bath through fired clay chimney pipes built into the walls of the building. In contrast to the Ottoman type, some very large Roman baths supplemented the heating with additional stokepits built below the bath floors.

Although the Ottoman baths employed the same kind of heating system as did the earlier Roman ones, Turkish style baths are also dissimilar in many ways. The primary difference grew out of a significant change in size. Roman baths were huge; their great size not having been matched by any culture or society since. Also, whereas hot and cold pools were considered essential components of the Roman baths, the Ottomans used pools only in their thermal baths for--according to Islam--still water is contaminated and therefore should not be used for washing the body. Ottomans entered a pool only for medical purposes and then after having washed thoroughly beforehand. Another difference between the two types is that the Ottoman bath, unlike the highly decorated Roman bath buildings, is relatively unadorned.

Although many bath ruins can be found in other parts of Turkey, traces of Roman or Byzantine baths in Istanbul are scant, the only candidates being two foundations which archaeologists suspect may have been baths. It is believed, however, that at least three Ottoman baths were all, or in part, constructed over pre-existing Byzantine era baths. A Byzantine tablet found beneath the building inscription of the Çardaklı Bath together with components such as the plan of the bath's hot area of a type never seen before in any other Ottoman bath, leads researchers to believe that the builders must have been influenced by a Byzantine bath previously extant on the same site.

The Architect Sinan's Hagia Sophia Bath is one of the most beautiful examples of Ottoman bath architecture. (right)

Entrance portico of the Hagia Sophia Bath. (below)

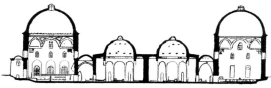

Most Ottoman baths are of the "double bath" type, so-called because of their mirrored plan, with twin men and women's facilities of the same size and structure. The other type of Ottoman bath, called the "single bath," consists of only one shared bathing facility reserved for the use of women during the day and for men during early morning hours, evenings, and nights. Most "double baths" have separate doors that open onto two different streets so that men and women do not have to meet each other on their way to or from the bath.

To simplify the heating of the "double baths," the two bathing sections were usually built side by side so that a single stokepit could be used to heat both sections. There are, however, exceptions to this rule in which the two bathing sections were built end to end. Designed to act as natural insulators to retain heat, the Ottoman baths were also con-structed of very thick walls, which provided the added advantage of strengthening the buildings, thereby increasing their resistance to natural disasters such as earthquakes.

Only a few Ottoman baths have inscription panels on their walls. The earliest example of a bath with such an inscription is the bath built in Mudurnu in 1382. The earliest Istanbul example is the magnificent Mahmut Paşa Bath constructed in 1467, a building still standing but no longer in use as a bath. The inscriptions usually give the construction date, the names of its sponsors, and sometimes various compliments about the bath and those responsible for its construction.

According to one of these inscriptions, cleanliness builds the character: "If you are a person of dirty morals and character, don't expect help from a bath. If you want to be clean, first clean your heart, then clean your body."

Most Ottoman baths have four major sections: the dressing room area, the warm area, the hot area and the stokepit. In most cases, the front section of the Ottoman bath has a porch-like entrance, this style inherited from the earlier Turkish Seljuk tradition. There are also a very few examples where the bath is entered directly via a door into the dressing room area. Most of these doors are decorated with very impressive stonework and date to the baroque period.

Dressing rooms are divided into two types: small dressing rooms with wooden dividing walls, and those built from brick or stone walls. The dressing room area represents the largest space in the bath itself, with its domed ceilings even larger and grander than those over the bathing area.

Although today serving as an exhibit hall, the best example of the large dome plan bath, the Hagia Sophia Bath built by the Ottoman's most famous architect, Sinan, has been restored to its original glory. Some of the other fine examples of the large dome plan baths still standing are the Çinili (tiled) bath also built by Sinan, the Çemberlitaş Bath, the Ortaköy Bath, the Kılıç Ali Paşa Bath, and the Süleymaniye Bath. According to various sources, in the first half of the 16th century the architect Sinan built between 15 to 29 public baths in Istanbul, in addition to the scores of baths he built within palaces and mansions. Sixteen of the Sinan baths are still standing, six of which are still being used as baths today.

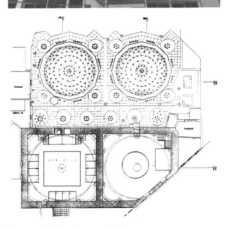

Examples from the Çemberlitaş Bath restoration project... Designed by architect Halil Onur, 3-D modeling by architects Ali Dereli and Onur Yalçın.

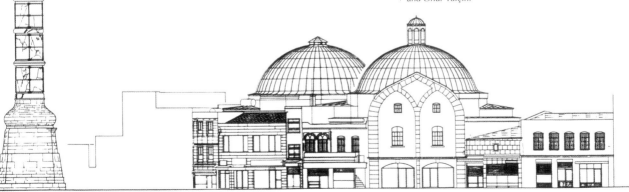

Other Ottoman baths with large domes were built in Anatolia before the Turks conquered Constantinople. Many of the baths of this era had domes with diameters averaging 10-15 meters. The dome covering the dressing rooms of the bath built in Mudurnu in 1382 spans twenty meters and is the largest dome of any Ottoman bath.

Although it no longer functions as a bath, the Mahmutpaşa Bath Building has the largest bath dome in Istanbul. The dome over its dressing room area has a diameter of 17 meters and is 27 meters high. The next largest is the Beyazıt Bath with a dome that is 15 meters across. Unfortunately, this building is in an advanced state of disrepair and hence no longer open to the public. Another large-dome type bath, the Kılıç Ali Paşa Bath, with a 14 meter diameter dome over its dressing rooms, is still in use. Because the roofs of many of these domes are covered in lead, they are called the "kurşunluk" (that which is of lead).

Cağaloğlu Bath, dressing room area (above)

Gedikpaşa Bath. The largest dome of any Ottoman bath (right).

The dressing room area generally consists of a large open space ringed with one to three tiers of small dressing rooms. The first baths built by the Ottomans did not have enclosed dressing cubicles. In the earliest examples of Ottoman bath architecture, this large open, common space was ringed with benches where the bathers undressed, rested on the benches, and hung their clothes. The private cubicles are later additions.

No matter how or when they were built, almost all of the wide-open spaces in the dressing section have a spraying water fountain in their very center. In the past this section also always had a marble tea preparation area. The incredibly beautiful stonework of these tea burners can still be seen in some baths today. As years passed, though, in many cases the special features of the wooden sections of the bath were not properly maintained, so were rebuilt or torn down completely.

The dressing rooms roofed with brick/stone domes are bathed in daylight that pours in through the "roof lantern." This "lantern" is a hexagonal or octagonal cupola rising from the center of the dome and ringed with windows. It was constructed of either wood or brick/stone. While most of these original elements

have, unfortunately, not been preserved, we can still see beautiful originals in the Çemberlitaş, Hagia Sophia and Süleymaniye baths.

As understood from its name, the warm area is a heated space, but one that never gets as hot as the "hot area." Like the hotter area, though, the walls and floor of this warm space are also covered in marble. The warm area is not used much, but those who cannot bear the temperatures of the hotter space, or the elderly, use this place for bathing. It is also used as a kind of "way station," where people gradually get used to the heat, or cool down after the bath. The warm area forms a longish rectangle. This space also has private bathing cubicles, marble benches for resting or massage, small cubicles used for shaving or depilatory body hair removal, and toilets.

The warm area leads to the hot bathing area via a door that is both narrow and low so as not to let the heat escape. The hot area is, of course, the hottest and most humid area of the bath. It is also very steamy due to the constant flow of the water and the window here that opens onto the hot water tank. The large marble-covered central stone, a large flat platform raised 45-50 centimeters off the floor and resting on a marble base, is the hottest area of the bath. Most of these central stones, used for resting and perspiring or for the massage, are octagonal or square in shape.

Vezneciler Bath's coffee preparation niche has incredibly fine stonework (above)

Hagia Sophia Bath fountain in the former dressing room area that is today used as an exhibit hall (left).

The walls of the hot area are lined with 70-100 cm wide marble partitions fitted with hot- and cold-water faucets. In front of the faucets are low marble stone stools. This area leads to small cubicles that offer even hotter washing opportunities. The name for these cubicles-helvet-derives from an Arabic word meaning "secluded or private place."

These cubicles are usually hotter than the general washing spaces and allow the bather to wash in private. Each cubicle has from one to three basins; they are usually not partitioned with doors, but those who wish may hang a pestemal over the entry for added privacy. In almost all of the baths operating today, the proprietors have walled off one or more of these cubicles to make a sauna. These sauna-cubicles have been lined with wood and doors, and heaters have been installed for extra heat and heat retention.

"Elephant eye" skylights catch the light from every direction (above and left).

The Beyazit Bath still awaits badly needed restoration, even though the restoration plan is complete (below).

The stone and mortar domes over the hot area of the bath are covered with lead on the exterior face. The central platform is illuminated by small, 15-20 centimeter diameter windows called "elephant's eyes" that are dotted over the dome. These windows are made of thick, bell-shaped glass that can catch the light from all directions. Either round or star-shaped (and sometimes both), these windows can catch whatever light is outside no matter what the hour of the day and send it filtering in a very mysterious and beautiful fashion over the bathers perspiring on the platform below. As the centuries have passed many of these elephant eye windows have been broken and today's bath proprietors tend to use flat, double-paned glass in their place, as custom-ordering the belled glass is frightfully expensive. Several of the best-preserved baths do retain the elephant's eyes though, so make sure you look up and enjoy the sight.

Ottoman bath plans follow older Anatolian forms. This bath has a central square-shape divided in the form of a cross with four eyvans, the three-sided antechambers seen so frequently in Ottoman architecture, in the central part of the outer square and the cubicles built around the corners. In this plan the antechambers and cubicles are raised higher than the central area. This same plan was often widely used by the Ottomans for medresse (teaching institutions) and home designs. Another plan type has a round hot area directly below the dome with the cubicles opening directly onto this area. This plan developed out of the Anatolian Roman bath and thermal bath styles and is seen more frequently in Ottoman thermal

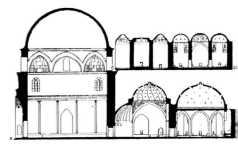

baths. Not all Ottoman baths are similar, though, and other, different architectural plans were also used during this period.

Historian and archaeologist Professor Dr. Semavi Eyice has carried out several very important research studies of Byzantine and Ottoman monuments and he has identified six main types of plans for Ottoman bath architecture. Eyice cataloged many of the baths existing in the Ottoman territories and then classified each according to this typography.

Crossection of the Mahmutpaşa Bath. Today this building is used as a shopping center (above).

Oftentimes the dressing room areas of the Turkish bath are illuminated by high skylights called sky lanterns (below).

A Type: This type has four eyvans and cubicles built in the corners. It is seen in approximately half of all baths catalogued, making it the most frequently used plan in the Ottoman period.

B Type: The periphery of the main central stones leads directly to the cubicles in a star shape. After "A" this is the second most frequently seen bath plan.

C Type: Domed cubicles are located on three sides of the square central stone.

D Type: A rectangular hot area is multi-domed with numerous arches.

E Type: The hot area is roofed with a number of small domes and this area opens onto two adjacent cubicle areas.

F Type: The warm area, hot area and cubicles are all built as same-size rooms and all are roofed with a number of small domes.

In days past the faucets were of brass and bronze but, today, most baths use home-type faucets. Those that try to attract tourists will still use brass faucets.

The marble kurna, sink-like basins directly under the faucets that collect just enough water for washing, are another intriguing feature of the Ottoman baths. These basins are used for collecting clean water only and are never defiled. They are made with incredibly fine stone workmanship and are a witness to the hand working skills of the past. It was also customary for the baths to maintain one very highly decorated marble basin called the "bride's basin." Many baths still retain the original basins and they are a delight to use and to admire.

The stokepit heats the building and the water used. It consists of a large fire pit built like a large furnace and topped with a grill. A large hot water tank made of either copper or steel sits over this grill. Ducts (called 'hellish paths') lead under the floor from this tank to the hot and warm areas. The heat and smoke that is transmitted through these ducts is then released to the outdoors via clay chimney pipes that reach the height of the outer surface of the domes.

The Ottoman baths are rather unadorned and plain when compared to the earlier Turkish Seljuk baths that used ceramic tiles for decoration. Some Ottoman baths did use tiles, though. Other decorative items include the beautifully worked stone armrests of the marble stools. If the bath used columns as supports these column heads were decorated in the "baklava" or stalactite style during the early Ottoman days and then in baroque style in later baths.

The cupolas (sky lanterns) of the Çemberlitaş Bath (left) and the Süleymaniye Bath (below).

The Essential Components of the Bath: Tellak and Natır

The male attendant at a Turkish bath is called a "tellak," while the female attendant is referred to as "natır." This is the person who washes you, gives you that deep scrub and the massage of a lifetime. This is the person who will slide you about, lift your arms and legs, and wash every part of your bodies--without ever touching your privates--with both flair and determination. Some of today's bath attendants, however, may wince when you call them by their rightful name as today both words are associated with a rather low occupation. Just as a "janitor" may today prefer to be called a "maintenance person," some "tellak" and "natır" may also prefer to be called masseusse. But even if the name has changed, the profession remains very much the same. Thank goodness!

Edouard Depat Ponsan, "Massage, Bath Scene," 1883.

Overseeing everything and everyone at the bath is the "hamamcı," the bathkeeper. In times of old he was a salaried professional, but now is the actual bath proprietor. Another staff member at the bath is the "külhancı" the keeper of the stokepit, the "külhan," and his helpers the "külhanbey." There is yet another person who has the job of greeting the customers at the door. He is called the "meydancı" or "keeper of the square." The "peshtemalcı" is, of course, the person responsible for handing out clean "peshtemals"--wrapping cloths--and ensuring that there are plenty on hand. Other jobs belong to the people who look after the dressing rooms, the "odacı" or "room keepers," and then there is the "yanaşma," the person whose job it is to run whenever anything is needed. The women's side has the same staff, the only difference being that they are all females. The supervisor of the female side is usually a close relative to the owner. The men feel that they can better control the operations of the "other" side if it is a family member who is overseeing the operations.

During the Ottoman period, baths played a very important role in everyday life and the tellaks were important personages. There were reportedly 2321 tellaks working in Istanbul baths at the close of the 17th century. This number did not

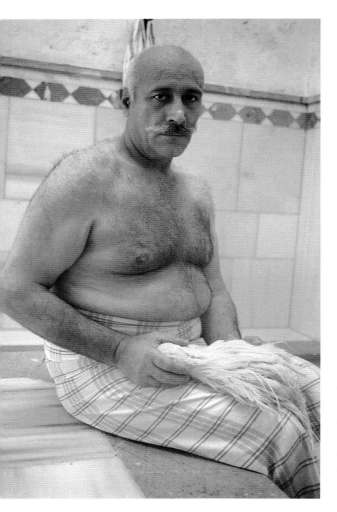

Ibrahim Çatalcam, a tellak from Tokat, works at the Örücüler Bath and continues the tradition of trade being passed down from grandfather to son to grandson.

include their female counterparts, the natır. We can probably correctly assume that this number rose in direct ratio to the increase of population in Istanbul in subsequent years.

The tellak community selected its apprentices from among young people who were 13-15 years of age. They expected these young people to have attractive features, and well-formed bodies and to be lively, active and good conversationalists. These recruits had to train within the Ottoman lonca tradition, a tradition of guilds that was based on very strict discipline. As was true for all of the professions, the apprentice had to spend many years training under the master or mistress before becoming a kalfa (journeyman) or assistant "tellak" or "natır." This promotion to kalfa represented a major step in the career. First the apprentice was wrapped in a black silk peshtemal. He or she first washed the hamancı or the mistress in one of the lower cubicles before being allowed to come to the main area to wash one of the bath's more prominent customers.

The kalfa became part of a strict hierarchy of discipline that rose up through the ranks to the end point, the proprietor. These tellaks did not receive a wage, but earned their living from the tips they received from customers. Usually they lived in common at the bath and shared their meals with one another, making it easier for them to get by. The tellak/natır apprentice system continued until 1908, the year that witnessed the modernization of the Empire with the enactment of constitutional reforms. A reform law forbade youths under the age of twenty from working as a tellak or natır, and any young tellaks under this age were immediately sent home. All tellaks and natırs had to obtain licenses from the local police and the law further required bi-monthly medical checkups. Only people of good morals could become attendants and anyone who had been arrested for rude behavior, sexual crimes, or resisting police were barred from the profession. Baths that did not comply could also be closed down.

During the Ottoman Empire, lonca (guild) activities were closely monitored and regulated, and various authorities--including police--were charged with overseeing these rules. According to lonca regulations of 1630, a tellak was required to be "good-looking, lively, active and clean shaven" and had to "maintain sharp razors, scrub and massage with powerful actions, wash the customer thoroughly with soap, and keep all scrubbing materials clean." Ten years later these regulations were expanded: "The tellak must drape a peshtemal around his neck when he is shaving the customer so that his perspiration does not drip onto the customer. After the customer is washed, the tellak must wrap him in a clean and dry peshtemal. The tellak must always wrap himself in a silk pestemal. Each customer may choose the tellak he prefers for scrubbing. The tellak must not look the customer in the eye after he has finished bathing as if to demand a tip. The amount of tip must be left to the generosity of the customer. After he has tipped, the customer should be offered some rose water cologne." After he washed the customer, the tellak was also charged with cleaning up the basin and other areas used by the customer. When the bath closed for the night, the entire bath and all the towels and peshtemals used that day had to be washed thoroughly.

Until the first quarter of the 18th century almost all of the tellaks were Albanians. The Tulip Period (1718-1730) was an era of extravagance as the empire began to put on a European face. Heavy taxes were levied to pay for all of this and soon the population joined forces in a general uprising led by an Albanian named Patrona Halil, a tellak who was then working in the Beyazıt Bath. This was to spell the end to the tradition of Albanian tellaks. Ahmed III was deposed by the rebels and replaced by Mahmut I. The new sultan was not grateful. He immediately had the rebel leaders--including Patrona Halil--executed. In 1734 a royal edict was sent to the Istanbul Kadı (courts) demanding that the name, legal record and physical appearance of every single employee in all baths in Istanbul, a list extending from the youngest apprentice to the most prestigious positions, be document-ed in special files. Albanian names were marked in red. The order also stipulated that no new tellaks could be Albanian. The existing Albanian tellaks were not fired from their jobs, but if any took leave to go to Albania to visit family, they were not reissued licenses upon their return. The edict clearly stated a preference for the replacement of Albanian telleks by Anatolian Turks and Greeks, and the bath managers were closely watched to make sure they complied with this order.

In the 18th century the centuries-

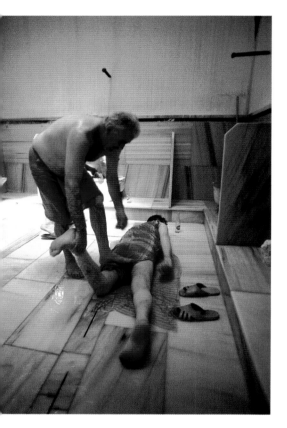

Tellaks traditionally come from the Eastern Anatolian towns of Tokat and Sivas.

long military arrangement began to break down. Members of the elite Janissary forces began to look for second jobs and some also worked as tellaks. Records show that members of the Janissary assigned to galleon, cannon, and armored battalions were also recorded as bath employees. In fact, Patrona Halil got his name from a ship called the Patrona, a ship on which he worked.

After the edict, the new Anatolian tellaks found their security in trustworthy numbers. They made sure that friends, relatives and neighbors were given the available jobs and, since that time, most tellaks have come from the neighboring towns of Sivas and Tokat in Central Anatolia. For centuries now these two provinces have remained at the very center of bath life and almost everyone working in the baths has some kind of familial relationship. In 18th and 19th century bath documents we find information regarding these two regions. An epic describing a bath writes, "Sivas is the home of the tellak/ the name of the clean tellak is spoken over the world." But while the bath proprietors and tellaks come from Sivas, their female counterparts, the natır, have usually been gypsy women. Through the centuries the profession of natır has passed down from woman to daughter or to daughter-in-law. While the black African population notable in Istanbul during the Ottoman Empire has today mostly been assimilated into the general population's gene pool, some records show that "Arab sisters" also worked as natırs.

Records show that thirty baths were built at various times within the Topkapı Palace complex. There was a strict hierarchy enforced in bath usage, with various baths being used by different echelons within the thousands of palace members and employees. The sultans usually bathed in the Hünkar (royal) Bath within the harem and were washed by their concubines. Some sultans, however, like Murat IV, bathed at the great central bath. Here he was washed by young tellaks chosen by the sultan himself or by some of the royal pages.

At that time there was a cadre of young tellaks assigned to wash these high-ranking officials and military officers. Janissary recruits were young boys from non-Moslem families who were selected to be trained at the palace to act as officials and officers of the empire. The palace "campaign dormitories" housed those of the recruits who were tasked with acting as pages to the sultan and the pashas when they went on military campaigns, or those young men who were being trained to be palace guards. These young men were given the best education and training the empire could provide, but they were also required to perform daily chores as a kind of payment for their keep. Thirty of these recruits were tasked to work as tellaks in the palace baths. These young men, whose ages ranged from 20-30, were called "barber boys," as they were also charged with barbering. The youths were sent to the baths on certain days according to their ranks and they worked at the bath both as tellaks and barbers. Each palace official had his own tellak who washed him personally.

Among these young tellaks were those who would later work their way up to very high positions of rank and power within the empire. One of these was Sokullu Mehmet Pasha, who became one of the most important personages in Empire history. Also among the famous from these ranks was Siyavush Pasha who was chosen by Murat IV in the 17th century to act as his private tellak in the royal bath.

Royal bath in the Topkapı Palace.

The Baths and Sex

Ottoman literature makes frequent mention of the relationship between the bath and homosexual practice. Homosexuality is and has been a reality in all societies throughout history. The Ottomans were no exception, of course, and homosexuality during the Ottoman era has been documented in various records.

During a time when it was forbidden, as obscene, for a woman to dance in public it was common for men to hire a young boy called a "köçek" to dance for them. Though quite rare today, there are some instances in Turkey where the "köçek" is still hired to dance. In Ottoman Turkish, the word for "using a boy", "oğlancılık" was used to describe homosexual acts. Some young tellaks also engaged in homosexual acts with their customers, or were used by customers for sexual pleasuring, and these young tellaks became the subjects of various poems and folk tales. While some have concluded this to mean that all tellaks were homosexual, this was not the case and homosexual practices at the bath were--and continue to be--the exception rather than the rule.

In 1685 a bath foreman named Dervish İsmail handwrote a work, Dellakname-i Dilkuşa (Pleasuring Tellak) that clearly describes the above. This book outlines the life stories and legends surrounding eleven of the most famous tellaks and also gives very revealing information about oğlancılık in the baths. The book is highly descriptive and even lists the prices charged by the tellak for either passive or active homosexual acts, all described in a very clear and straight-forward manner.

Dervish İsmail starts his book as follows, "I wrote this book upon the enticement and teasing of an attractive lover, a lover whose beauty is wondrous and unique. The most honorable name of that young man is Yemenici Bali, a personage whose beauty is the jewel in his crown, a lad whose sable eyebrows are the very object of this sinner's desire." He then continues, "One day Yemenici Bali told me, 'Master, each day is followed by a night. What if the work we do pleas-uring others could be described in a little book? And what if--after we are long gone--this book were to remain as a memory of who we were and what we did?' And thus did he entice me and so I began to write." Dervish Ismail then goes on to describe the stories of eleven famous tellaks of the day and the conditions under which they worked. He details how some tellaks received money in return for

Ottoman–style miniature depicting a men's bath.

sexual favors and relates that there was a market for these kinds of activities. All in rhymes which we cannot do justice to here, he describes Yemenici Bali thus: "He has beauty, grace, manners and a good education and is refined and loyal. He's a rosebud on the branch of love and has a baby nightingale fluttering in his breast. His hair is a hyacinth, his dimple a rose, his look is cruel, his height a boxwood tree, his tummy a drop of light, his calves silver columns, his feet silver ingots, and his locks are silk threads." He gushed, "Bali was once an apprentice to a scarf maker in Tophane, but now the dainty boy struts around the garden like a peacock in his clogs." He continued, "There is a saying about the Janissary seamen, 'One eats, while the other looks on, and that's where the trouble starts.' And that's what happened. One night they flocked around Bali like bees around a honeycomb and though his name should be written in gold, they chose copper. Bali under-stood that it was time for him to go to the baths so he went to the seamen's bath at Tophane, kissed the hands of the head tellak, and started to work there. He charges 70 akçe. For 20 akçe more he will bring another tellak. He charges 300 akçe for a night on a mattress. He never accepts more than three customers a day. He's a clean and sound nightingale for the soul."

Another tellak that Dervish Ismail describes at some length is Hamleci (rower) İbrahim. "He's the light of our eyes, tall as a sapling, with the traits of an angel; the locks on his cheeks are golden threads; he has a narrow waist, and dainty hands and feet; his lips are a perfect rose; his tummy is a flower, a hyacinth. He's a sip of cool water. When he reclines on the turquoise mattress he has spread on the white marble floor of a private cubicle he imparts new life into another life. He only works with the most elite and gets 200 kurush each time he does. He gets 1000 kurush for a night on the mattress, and 250 kurush for providing extra services."

In addition to this book there was another written by Firuz Shah, also known as Little Red Lamb Firuz. In his work Firuz describes the stories of "Girlish" Softa, Calvary Mustafa Bey, Groom Ali, Suleyman the Sailor, Black Mole Davut, Gold-headed İskender, Cashmere Mustafa and Carnation Hasan.

Fuzuli, the famous Ottoman poet of the 16th century, praised the tellak who shaved him with, "Daylight has broken and the beauty has sharpened his blade / The sun shines on the sword showing its loyalty to the moonlike tellak / He starts...and from the swish-swish of his amber aroma blade / I come clean in the joy of bubbles from blade laps into the water / If there was a head at the tip of each strand and my lover chopped off each one like hair / Still I would not run from the blade spilling my blood." In another epic written by an unknown poet about the Şengül Bath, the poet describes a tellak and says that, "indeed, the kissing of feet must be a sinful pleasure" and then writes of "retiring to the silver-edged house (the private cubicle) with the doe-eyed tellak". The same epic also speaks of a tellak who "pounces like a tiger, whose clogs should be the crown on everyone's head, and who teases all with his dagger-like stare." In a 150 couplet bath epic written by Tosyalı Aşık Mustafa in the 19th century, he describes the tellak as "a silver cypress in front of each basin / cheek fire burning on the white marble / some build up and others tear down / a house of love that makes and breaks.' Also in the 19th century Aşık (bard) Veysel wrote a 20-couplet poem about the Grand Bath of Üsküdar. He describes the tellaks there as, "I don't know if they're twins or just the same age / and I can't say they're more than 15 / But they're unique for their coquettish airs and polite refinement / the kind that you will only find at a very special bath.' In the mid 19th century upon the restoration of the Çinili Bath, its proprietors, following tradition, commissioned a folk poet to write a poem to commemorate the occasion. The poet complimented the bath's ten tellaks with, "At your service, a fairy-faced creature / a fugitive from heaven."

Turkey's famous historian, Reşat Ekrem Koçu, wrote in the "dellak" section of his Istanbul Encyclopedia, a book that though unfinished, is full of interesting facts and details. "Beautiful boys of between 13-15 entered the life and spent years among men whose status and prestige far surpassed them. They walked

around entirely naked with only a silk peshtemal for covering, beckoning great adventures in the fantasies of those that saw them." He also wrote that some of the tellaks received very generous tips for some of the weighty services they performed. All sex at the bath was not homosexual though. An Ottoman entry records that the authorities demolished a male bath that hired women as tellaks, as such a practice represented unfair competition to other baths.

The "kese," a rough cloth that is used to wipe away dead skin cells, is an indispensable part of the Turkish bath tradition.

Another interesting document written in 1810 (a time when the Janissary military system had begun to fall apart) describes how the soldiers attached to the Janissaries began to pose problems for the city of Istanbul. It seems that a group of Janissaries who were posted at a local police station and charged with keeping the order, instead raided the Çemberlitaş Bath and kidnapped a young tellak, supposedly to have him dance for them. This led to a public outcry and a second Janissary police station had to be called in. When an armed battle between the two Janissary groups seemed imminent, the leading Janissary officers intervened, arrested the offenders and released the young man. The matter was settled when ten of those who had been involved in the kidnapping were hanged the next day in front of the bath.

A newspaper article written at the close of the 19th century states that a "slow-witted" man named Malatyalı Halil went to a bath in Samsun. It seems Halil was attracted to a tellak at this bath but this tellak always rebuffed his favors. Angered, Halil attacked and wounded the tellak with his dagger. He then stabbed himself twice in the abdomen with this same dagger, "disemboweling himself of all his own stupidity." The newspaper went on to report that there were several "oğlan" tellak working in baths in Samsun and Trabzon and that the men in these two towns were spending most of their money on these young men and "like cockroaches, once they go to the baths never want to come out again." The women of the two towns complained that their men were completing ignoring them and not looking after their children. These women reportedly wrote petitions asking the authorities to "put an end to this improper activity."

Following the constitutional reform of 1908 the city inspectors forbade any tellaks of any age, not just those under the age of twenty, from selling sexual favors at a bath. The regulation also required all tellaks to be examined every two months to determine whether that person had a sexually transmitted disease.

The history of sex in the Ottoman bath differs greatly from the general western impression of the Turkish bath as representing the "mystique of the harem." And while there was some sex at the bath (usually same sex), this was the exception and far from the rule. Some mistakenly believe that the Turkish bath was a place for group sex and that people of both sexes bathed together. Some "tourist" baths--usually located at resorts--support the myth by providing tourists with "mixed baths." This is unfortunate as it does great injustice to the essence of the Turkish bath and may be a ploy to humiliate women. Be forewarned and use your common sense!

Tellak: Then and Now

In the past the tellak would make their soap sudsy by whisking the bar of soap in a deep copper basin with a special brush made of the fibers of date tree roots. They would also use a rough black haircloth to give the customer a deep scrub. Today the tellak uses a plastic pan, woven washcloths and scrubbing cloths made of textile fibers.

The clogs, peshtemal, copper basin and date root whisk were provided by the bath, while the tellak had to provide his own haircloth scrubbers. That's why, when a tellak was fired from a bath he was told to "take his scrubbers and go."

During the Ottoman period it was strictly forbidden for the tellaks and customers to use the same kind of peshtemal. The customers wrapped in peshtemals with a white background, woven with red, violet, or yellow, while the tellak wore plain black silk, a peshtemal that inspired many poems. Today both customers and tellaks and natırs wear the same kind of peshtemal, a wrap made from a tightly woven fabric that is ideal both for covering the body and absorbing moisture. These peshtemals are usually red plaid over a beige or yellow background.

Copper pouring bowl and a whisk made of date root fibers.

THE STAR OF THE TURKISH BATH: Külhanbeyi

He wore a close-fitting wine-colored fez, bellbottom trousers and a light colored shirt topped with an open vest; he had a pocket watch with a long chain that dangled over one trouser pocket and a large knife called a saldırma (attacker). His jacket was draped over his shoulders-never worn. On his feet he wore pointed shoes with egg-shaped heels and with the backs pressed down. walked like a crab, and he would shout out with a particular sound --Hey EYYYH!-- to let people know he was approaching.

This is the külhanbey, a personage famous in novels, plays, and film. He has been portrayed so frequently that even today everyone automatically recognizes "the külhanbey type." However, ask anyone just where this figure comes from and you are unlikely to receive a confident reply for, despite a career that goes back at least a hundred years, few people know the exact roots of this character, which is so embedded in the cultural fabric of Turkey that he has become a virtual stereotype.

Actually, the külhanbey type and name originate from the culture and traditions of the Ottoman bath. The furnace of the bath, or the huge stokepit where the fire is built, is called the külhan (literally ash house) and the person who tends the fire is the külhancı.

Thick tree logs were used to fuel the stokepit as these would keep the fires going for a long period. The külhancı was responsible for everything related to the fire, from buying the wood and transporting it to the bath, to lighting the fire and keeping it going. The külhan had to be lit every day, winter and summer, and it had to be kept alight day and night. The rule remained strictly imposed: the fire could never be allowed to go out.

It was hard work for the külhancı to do this all by himself, so he would find homeless children or orphans to help him keep the fire going, to haul the heavy logs off the wagon, stack them, throw them onto the fire, and then later empty the külhan of their ashes. Merely finding a warm place to sleep represented a great opportunity. The baths were huge structures, so these homeless children had no problem finding a space in which to bed down. The arrangement was ideal for the proprietor as well, for the children were willing to work for free. But while they constituted free labor for the bath, the children still had to find another way to earn their bread. They did this by begging, stealing, or by organizing the "bag" gambling tricks. On the streets they were considered to be toughs and hoodlums. The word "bey" means "gentleman" and it is generally considered that they were called külhanbey with satiric recognition of their low status and rough behavior.

Close family members could cause problems so the külhancı generally preferred to take in orphans among the ranks of children. As was true for initiation into any of the trade organizations (the loncas or guilds of the Ottoman period), entering the külhan also meant that the recruit had to adhere to strict practices and traditions. Most importantly, any of the children or youths of a külhan had to recognize and obey the authority of the külhancı. A disobedient child would immediately be thrown out. Every ten children in any given külhan were the direct responsibility of an older, more experienced külhanbey, a youth called a "destebaşı," the "head of ten."   This "head" was responsible for the everyday life of the youths under his charge.

The tradition called for the new recruit to a külhan to provide all of the other külhanbeys in that bath with the ingredients to cook halvah and a pilaf. He had to do this by begging in the local marketplace. This first experience at begging marked a kind of trial by fire, as the others in the külhan determined whether he had the wit and the determination to be a good beggar.

Everyone shared the pilaf and halvah--as was common practice when it came to food--that was served that night by the newcomer. The actual ceremony, however, began after the meal had been eaten. At this point, the külhancı picked up a small piece of bread that he dipped into salt. He then recited the külhan pledge: "This place is a true külhan / The home of the homeless and the poor / Many brave men were trained here / Who knows where they are today / Children are the guests of this külhan / Our leader is the Great Layhar / He that does right is a sultan in his own right / Let us all shout "hu" in memory of Layhar / HU! / Poor or rich were all the same to him." Each külhanbey would then recite the same lines in turn. The leader, the Great Layhar, was supposed to have lived during the time of Ghazneli Mahmud. He was called Layhar (mud drinker) because he drank wine dregs and he was the symbol of rude behavior and acting "overly familiar." Because they so rudely demanded food and drink from the market keepers, the külhanbeys too were stamped with the reputation of their so-called leader.

Each newcomer to the külhan was assigned a "brother," from among the other newcomers. A ceremony of "brotherhood" was also held in the külhan to mark this relationship. The boys who were to become "brothers" would strip naked and stand side by side. They were wrapped in a large white shirt called "Layhar's shroud." Each child put one arm into one of the sleeves of the shirt. The külhancı would then recite, "The külhan is neither mine nor yours. Those who are brothers here are closer than those born of the same mother and father. Each day they will bring their earnings to the külhan and will cook and eat together." The entire group would then join in a prayer of remembrance for their leader Layhar, the members of the külhan would welcome the newcomer, and the two "brothers" would sleep together that night, still sharing the same shirt. There was a hierarchy in sleeping area. The longer a child was at the külhan, the closer he got to sleep to the furnace, especially in winter. Children who were sick, however, were always moved close to the furnace to keep them warm.

The külhanbeys were a cosmopolitan group, reflecting the colorful ethnic and religious makeup of the city, but no matter their background, all boys lived together in a family-like atmosphere. The külhanbeys formed a close unit, sharing with and taking care of each other. In the evening they shared whatever they had at a common meal. Residents in the neighborhood would often provide the children with leftovers from their own kitchens and other kind-hearted souls would bring food to the külhan. The younger children either begged in the street or hired themselves out to carry market parcels

From the archives of Ergun Hiçyılmaz.

from the markets to the shoppers' homes. As they got older, the boys usually turned to thieving, pickpocketing, taking protection money or working as paid bullies. Some of the young men registered with the fire brigade as volunteer firemen who would join a specific "fire brigade hearth." They would then get a share of the payment given to the brigade by the person who had suffered the fire. At one point in time, the külhanbeys worked as volunteer street sweepers receiving (or extracting) payment from the residents of the particular street. However, if payment was not readily forthcoming, the residents might find more mud than usual on their street, spread by the külhanbeys in retaliation for "unpaid bills."

While the külhanbeys harassed shop owners and street peddlers, they scrambled for money by running to help the volunteer fire brigade, or offering to help load bearers or women and children who seemed to be in need of assistance. Rich children, butchers and coal sellers were frequent butts of their teasing and many of the "goodly" population despaired of ever teaching them to be responsible citizens. These boys were considered so unsavory that the local judges--the kadı-- went so far as to issue an edict forbidding the young bath attendants from befriending any of the külhanbey boys.

The külhanbey had their own dialect of slang, "külhanbey mouth," that included at least 200-300 words not used by the general population. In the 19th century, a broadsheet listed 80 words unique to the külhanbey culture. Newcomers to the külhan were taught these words so that the boys could communicate with one another in a way that was unintelligible to the uninitiated. Their language

Drawings by Derya Sayın

also represented their lifestyle. They called their külhancı "father," and the mosque courtyard "home." Some of this slang vocabulary has been preserved and it is still used by people today. Turks call a person who chatters too much a "goose," an unsavory person "satan," a clumsy person "gimpy," an ill person a "lozenge," and acting crazy "scratching at the door," all külhanbey expressions.

As their numbers and illegal activities increased, the authorities tried to bring the külhanbeys under their control. Sultan Selim III, of the 18th century, was renowned for traveling about in disguise to check whether his edicts were being enforced. Following one of these excursions, he issued an edict ordering that other boys not be allowed to associate with the külhanbeys, who were often in trouble and often getting dragged off to the local police station where they would be soundly beaten and released. However, society was beset with problems and it was almost impossible to stanch the flood of young men into the streets. The police decided to stamp out these gangs of youths once and for all. On a night in 1846, the police raided all of the baths in Istanbul, gathering up all the children they found there, nearly 800 külhanbeys. The police announced that henceforth no children were to be sheltered in the baths. Those over the age of 16 were taken into the army and those under that age were forced to work in the army shoe factory. The külhanbeys who were enlisted in the army easily rose through the ranks as they were experienced in the skills desired by the military. One of these boys--Külhan Rıza--even rose to the rank of general.

The police actions put an end to the tradition and institution of the külhanbeys. But while the tradition died out, the reputation of the külhanbey character grew into a stereotype and has remained very much alive. Having become mythical figures, they are remembered today as the young man who harasses the neighborhood guard, the rebel who terrorizes the neighborhood while also being its most staunch protector, the guy on the block who protects the honor of all of the women in the district from being bothered by a "stranger,"- all in all, the portrait of a kind of urban Robin Hood. The people's feelings about this kind of young man are probably best summed up by the short couplet: "Should I call him a provincial boor, a flea-ridden menial? Or should I call him the vagabond of the bath's külhan?"

Today most Turks might not be able to tell you what a külhan is, but everyone can describe the character of a külhanbey and know that he was some kind of star of the Ottoman bath.

A Guide to the Historic
Turkish Baths of Istanbul

In the Bath...

Check the hours of operation of the baths in this guide. When you enter a bath, first check out the prices posted and then find out whether the price includes the scrub and massage. These two services are optional. There is always an English-speaking person available at any bath that we have recommended. Remember that any difference between the fee charged for Turks and that charged for "tourists" is not because of a desire to "cheat the tourist," but rather to ensure that the attendants get paid. The various attendants at the bath do not earn a salary, but, rather, make their living through tips. This is an accepted part of Turkish tradition and Turks pay a tip for each "service" they receive. While there is indeed a posted price for deep scrub and massage, the attendants who perform these services will expect a tip--from Turks and foreigners alike--in addition to the posted price. Through the years both bath proprietors and attendants have learned that tourists are not aware of this tradition and so they post two bath schedules to ensure that they and the attendants are paid for services rendered. The bath will try to charge you one basic fee that will include all the services like deep scrub and massage and the expected tip. The total charged for the tourist, however, usually includes a very generous tip, one that even many Turks might not pay.

Bargain! Just as you would in any shop in the Covered Bazaar! After you have agreed on a price, you will be shown to your private changing room. Here you will remove all of your clothes and cover yourself in the wrap, the peshtemal, that has been provided for you. Men must be wrapped from the waist down, whereas women may either wrap from the waist down, or in a manner that will conceal their breasts. Those who prefer may also enter the bath dressed in a bathing suit. The men's bath tends to be more modest than the women's. Women are freer in terms of removing or loosening wrappings to wash, but it is strictly forbidden in all baths for men to open or remove their peshtemal. Some baths even post warning signs to this effect.

The key to the dressing room is in the lock. Lock the door and take the key with you to the bathing area. Some baths provide small lockers in the entry hall for customers to store their valuables. If you use a locker keep the key with you. Signs will inform you that the bath is not responsible for items not secured. The best thing is not to take large sums of money, jewellery or other valuables (including passports) with you to the bath. If you must carry such items, give them to the proprietor for safekeeping.

As you walk into the hot bathing area, the attendant will ask whether you want a scrub and massage. Traditionally, the bather either requests neither or will ask for both, but it is always possible to ask for only one or the other. Twenty to thirty minutes after you have rested in the hot area, the attendant will appear to begin to wash you. There are no set times in the bath, however, and you can request this service whenever you want. You are entirely free to spend as much or as little time in any of the bathing activities, sitting in the sauna, relaxing on the central stone, washing, etc. The bath proprietors will never pressure you in this regard.

If you want to use the sauna you should ask if one is available before entering the bath. Because the saunas are wood-covered, you should first wash and then request a new, dry peshtemal before entering the sauna. A dry peshtemal is also needed if you are going to lie on the central stone. Most baths also keep pumice stones available for those who want to remove corns or dry skin as the moist climate of the bath is ideal for this. Feel free to ask an attendant to bring you a pumice stone (ponza).

The temperature of a Turkish bath will range between 35-45°C depending on the season. The temperature in a sauna usually ranges from 55-60°C.

The attendants in a women's bath are always female, while those in the male bath (and the rare and very untraditional mixed baths offered tourists) are male. The attendant will first use a thick, deep-scrubbing mitt worn on the right hand to give you a deep scrub to remove all dirt from within the cells. Dead skin cells will be sloughed off in another full washing. Following this deep scrub and thorough washing, you will lie on a dry peshtemal spread over the central stone and be given a massage, the kind of massage that is the calling card of the Turkish bath. This massage is deeply relaxing as your muscles are now completely loose in this warm and moist atmosphere. Relax and let the attendant move you about freely. Once accustomed to the massage, you will get an appreciation for the acclaim of the Turkish bath.

After the massage the tellak will leave you wrapped in a towel and peshtemal and will wish you good health--"sıhhatlar olsun." The bather is now free to stay in the bath for as long as desired. The bather should find a deserted corner to wrap up in yet another dry peshtemal before now moving to the "warm" space. An attendant waiting here will immediately offer you a new dry towel. Yet another dry towel will be offered as you head to the dressing room. Once in the dressing room you are now totally relaxed and clean. You can rest on the cot, can enjoy a hot or cold beverage and even take a nap. No one would ever disturb you.

The baths we have recommended also have hair dryers. Some baths will polish your shoes without your requesting the service, but they will expect a small tip

in return. If you agreed on a set price for all the services you want when you first entered the bath then you will not be expected to tip. You may tip, of course, if you were very pleased with the service.

Shoes can also be shined at some baths.

The Bath and Health

Turkish baths are almost always housed in large and spacious buildings. Despite this, the high temperatures and constant use of hot water combine to create a high humidity atmosphere, one to which the body is not accustomed. The conditions here raise body temperatures, setting almost all the organs of the body into action as they expend energy. This, in turn, is very beneficial to the body.

Resting in a place that is very hot and humid, then having the body deep scrubbed, followed by a thorough washing with lots of soapy suds all work together to help the body slough off its dead skin cells and promote the growth of new cells. Since it takes, on an average, three weeks for the replacement of our outer skin cells, the speeding up of this process at the bath helps to keep the skin alive and healthy.

For thousands of years physicians have understood the positive effect that heavy perspiration can have on a person's well-being and this very human act is used in many cases as a medical treatment. Perspiring is as important to the body as breathing. A person who rests for fifteen minutes in a hot sauna, cubicle or on the main stone will expel 1.5 liters of perspiration. Heavy perspiration is said to ease the work of the kidneys. Ten percent of the content of perspiration is made up of unwanted substances. Over time, air pollution and other factors, such as wearing synthetic fabrics, will act to clog our pores, making it more difficult for our bodies to perspire. The heavy perspiration that we experience in the baths completely solves this problems. The opening of our pores in the bath is helpful to the treatment of skin blemishes and cellulite problems. By perspiring we get rid of the toxic substances in our body, act to balance body temperature, and deep clean our skin. Perspiration also helps the body expel the lactic acids that are a source of muscle pain. Our muscles also relax in the hot bath, along with the heavy perspiration. The elderly often experience difficulty perspiring and so, if they are not suffering from any diseases that would prevent them from attending the baths, a visit to the Turkish bath can be very helpful in this regard. Bath-induced perspiration is also very helpful to those suffering from the flu, arthritis, headache, or those with a hangover. In Turkey it is common that those who find themselves too intoxicated to go home will go to a bath where they will sleep till morning. Then in the early morning they will take a bath that will both sober them up and get rid of the hangover.

The hot and humid climate of the bath increases the body's need for oxygen, thus activating the respiratory system and increasing breathing rate. The heart conforms to this acceleration and also begins beating faster. This, in turn, speeds up the flow of blood through the body, supporting the body's defense systems. The increase in heart rate may constitute a risk for those who suffer from heart disorder or hypertension, and we suggest that those with these physical complaints consult their physician before going to a bath. Physicians also do not recommend the bath for those who suffer from chronic respiratory ailments. Those with open sores should also consult a doctor before washing at a bath as the hot and humid climate may make it easier for the person to get an infection through the

skin opening. The heat of the bath may also trigger a migraine in people who suffer from such problems.

Those individuals with weak immunity systems should rest at least 10-15 minutes in the warm area before moving into the hot area or before moving back to the area of normal temperature. This precaution is why Turkish baths have this warm area.

Baths collect their water in large storage tanks where it may stand for a long time. It is essential, therefore, that the water flowing from bath pipes not be drunk. You may bathe in the water with no fear of ill health, but drinking or swallowing the water may cause intestinal problems.

The bath will provide you with a small bar of soap to be used for a single bathing, but bring any other essentials you will want to use. Do not worry about the cleanliness of the peshtemals and towels at any of the baths we have recommended for they are all extremely clean and hygienic and can be used without hesitation.

Turkish baths have marble floors. Because these floors are wet they may also be highly slippery. The wooden slippers and clogs that were used in the bath have mostly given way to plastic slippers, even though a few baths still use wooden clogs for safety. Wooden clogs are heavy, however, so take care if you are using them for the first time and make sure that your foot doesn't slip out of them.

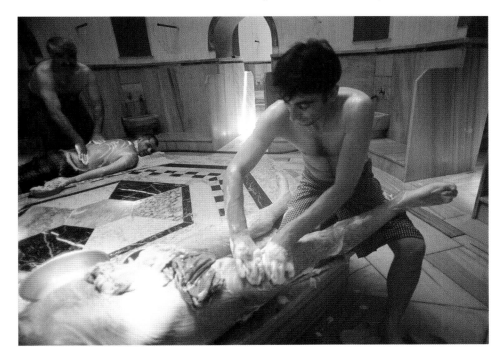

The deep scrub and massage are essential elements of a Turkish bath.

Çemberlitaş Bath

This bath was commissioned in 1584 by Nurbanu Sultan, mother of Sultan Murat III, to generate funds to support the külliye (complex of buildings composed of schools, a mosque, asylum for the mentally ill, hospital, soup kitchen) of Atik Valide Sultan. It is located in Çemberlitaş Square overlooking the "Burnt Column' (as it is called in English), which gives the square its name. The exquisite building was created by Mimar (Architect) Sinan, the architect who gave us the most outstanding examples of Ottoman architecture. This bath is near other important historical buildings, such as the tomb of Mahmut the Second, the Köprülü Library, and the Atik Ali Paşa Mosque.

The Çemberlitaş was originally built as a double bath, with separate facilities for men and women, and, even though for certain periods it stopped being used this way, today it again serves in this capacity. Part of the women's section was demolished in the second half of the nineteenth century during construction of a road. This section was then replaced by shops that are still in use to this day. This major change resulted in the use of the same entrance by women and men, a feature not characteristic of Ottoman bath architecture. There is an original six-line inscription over its entrance.

Originally, both men and women's sections were roofed by graceful cupolas (called roof lanterns in Turkish) but today only the women's section has this beautiful feature. Over the changing rooms of both the men's and the women's sections there are broad domes that are eighteen meters high. On leaving the changing rooms, one passes through the warm area roofed by three domes. The "hot" bathing section, square in plan from the outside, deviates from traditional Ottoman architecture with a 12-cornered plan formed by twelve columns. The four middle sections each have four private cubicles. These private cubicles are walled by marble dividers inscribed with verses. The marble floor is decorated with colored stone and the bath boasts a central heating stone that is larger than any other in Istanbul.

During the First World War the Çemberlitaş Bath was used for steam disinfecting procedures for the military hospital. The bath underwent major repair in 1972-

73 but a new restoration project is currently being planned.

The Çemberlitaş Bath is one of the cleanest and best maintained of the few recommended baths of Istanbul. Its location, and the efficiency and attitude of its management make it very popular for tourists. Among the reasons for its popularity is that its staff almost all speak English and the bath accepts credit cards as payment. The bath also gives discounts to tourists with International Student Cards, to Turkish students living in dormitories, and to steady customers. Included in the entrance fee is insurance in the unlikely case of accident during the time the customers use the facilities.

Address	Vezirhan Cad. No: 8 Çemberlitaş-Eminönü
Telephone	(0 212) 520 18 50–520 15 33
Fax	(0 212) 511 25 35
Web Site	http://www.cemberlitashamami.com.tr
e-mail	contact@cemberlitashamami.com.tr
Hours of Operation	06:00-24:00
Price	15 Euros
	Women-Men

Cağaloğlu Bath

The Cağaloğlu Bath is located in the historical center of Sultanahmet, the district in which countless buildings and museums such as the Hagia Sofia, the Blue Mosque, Topkapı Palace and the Yerebatan Cisterns draw huge numbers of tourists, foreign and domestic. The Cağaloğlu Bath not only ranks as the last big bath to be built in Istanbul, but it also is a gem in its own right, displaying all the beauties of traditional "bath architecture."

The bath's original inscription is still very readable in its spot over the entrance. The inscription tells us that the bath was built as a "double bath" in 1741 by the sultan of the time, Mahmut I, who had it constructed as a means of providing maintenance funds for the Hagia Sofia Mosque. It is thought that the plans were

drawn by Head Architect Suleiman Agha, but that the construction was actually completed by Abdullah Agha. The Cağaloğlu Bath still serves both women and men as originally intended. The men's dressing area, entered through a marble door decorated in a style not typical of early Ottoman baths, is not only spacious but also well lit by the roof lantern in the center of the dome. There are two tiers of clean and well-kept dressing rooms in this section, where both the large and impressive fountain with its pool and the capitals of the columns are decorated in baroque style.

The heated section occupies a special place in Ottoman bath architecture. It is square in plan and has eight marble columns with carved capitals. There are three antechambers, or eyvans, a typical Ottoman architectural device that resembles a kind of portico and that may also be referred to as an exedra, four bathing cubicles and an octagonal central stone with sloping sides. One of the cubicles that faces the antechambers has been converted for use as a sauna, an interesting conversion for, as is typical of Ottoman bath architecture, it has no door.

The baroque style of the bath's architecture shows the beginning of the foreign influence in Ottoman architecture. The building itself was completed just before the 1786 royal decree that forbade the construction of any more public baths due to shortages of water and firewood. The Cağaloğlu Bath is one of the best of the clean, well-kept and recommended baths in Istanbul. It is efficiently managed and is staffed by personnel who speak English. The bath also has a bar-restaurant that is entered through the men's dressing room. This dining spot is highly popular and reservations are recommended. Credit cards are honored.

Address	Prof. Kazım İsmail Gürkan Cad. No: 34 Cağaloğlu-Eminönü
Telephone	(0 212) 522 24 24
Fax	(0 212) 512 85 53
Web Site	http://www.cagalogluhamami.com.tr
e-mail	info@cagalogluhamami.com.tr
Hours of Operation	Open every day; Women: 08:00-20:00 / Men: 07:00-22:00
Price	20 Euros
	Women-Men

Örücüler Bath

Another of the public baths that can be recommended to the public as clean and well-kept is the Örücüler Bath. This bath is located in Beyazıt near the Örücüler or "Weavers'" Gate of the Covered Bazaar. It is also called the "Back Bath" because most of its customers were the porters who worked near this gate carrying bundles on their backs. The precise date of its construction is not known, but it is known to have been built before the year 1489 by the Fatih Mosque Foundation. Since it is located right beside the Covered Bazaar, it is a popular tourist attraction. It has clean dressing rooms, a beautifully decorated roof lantern set in the wooden roof, a carved marble tea-cooking area dating from 1833, and wall tiles (added after the original construction) covering the area above the entrance-door. The heated section includes five cubicles and two rectangular main stones. The dressing rooms are clean and well looked after and the bath is well managed.

Address	Kapalıçarşı Örücüler Kapısı Sok. No: 32 Beyazıt-Eminönü
Telephone	(0 212) 527 92 63
Hours of Operation	06:00-23:00
Price	10 Euros
	Men Only

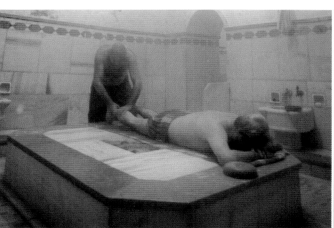

Süleymaniye Bath

The Süleymaniye Bath was built as part of the Süleymaniye Mosque and its complex in 1557 by the architect Sinan, who claimed the Süleymaniye Mosque--considered one of the two biggest and most beautiful of Istanbul's mosques--to be his masterpiece. The beauty and spaciousness of the Süleymaniye Bath reflects Sinan's genius as well. In Ottoman times, this bath was also called the "Metal Workers" Bath, because of its then proximity to the foundries. Sinan lived in a house next to the Süleymaniye Complex, and even today the bath continues to preserve the private cubicle he used for bathing from 1557 when the bath was built until his death in 1588. A piece of a coffee cup believed to have been used by Sinan was also

preserved in the bath for hundreds of years. At one time, there is also said to have been a special pouring basin used by Sinan. Also preserved for hundreds of years, this basin, now lost, was believed to have cured jaundice when used to pour water over a sick person's body.

The bath was originally opened by Sultan Süleyman the Magnificent, and the private cubicle he used was later set aside for the exclusive use of the highest ranking theological scholars. Both Süleyman's and Sinan's cubicles are still preserved. Over the centuries, the bath has been used mostly by the students from the medrese, the Islamic theological college.

Because of the prevalence of historical objects and structures throughout the area, the integrity of the Süleymaniye Bath and its environs--a bath more fortunate than many other public baths--has been preserved without any major modifications or additions. The only modification has been the 19th century addition of private dressing cubicles in the dressing area. The spacious and beautifully illuminated heated section is made up of three vaulted eyvans or antechambers and four cubicles. The central stone is surrounded by eight very striking marble columns connected by arches. After being privately owned for many years and not used as a bath, it was restored to function as a tourist bath in 2001 when it was taken over by the General Directorate of Foundations. The water supply still comes from the well that was dug when the structure was originally built.

This bath is also one of the baths in Istanbul to be recommended as clean and well-maintained.

Address	Mimar Sinan Cad. No: 20 Beyazıt-Eminönü
Telephone	(0 212) 520 34 10
Web Site	http://www.suleymaniyehamami.com
e-mail	contact@suleymaniyehamami.com
Hours of Operation	06:00-24:00
Price	15 Euros
	Open for men or mixed tourist groups

Şifa Bath

The Şifa Bath is in the Sultanahmet area, adjacent to the Nakilbend Mosque. It is thought to have been built sometime before 1715 by the Ömer Efendi Foundation, which was established by an imperial physician of the 18th century to raise revenue for the theological school built by the same person.

The original dressing area, entered through a long corridor, has unfortunately lost its original construction and design. The baroque style fountain and door in this section still retain, though, a certain beauty. The heated section is made up of three vaulted, three-sided antechambers and 2 private rooms.

Address	Şifa Hamamı Sok. No: 26 Sultanahmet-Eminönü
Telephone	(0 212) 638 38 49
Hours of Operation	06:00-24:00
Price	10 Euros
	Men Only

Gedikpaşa Bath

Located beside the Gedikpaşa Mosque, near Beyazıt Square, the Gedikpaşa Bath is one of the biggest and oldest of Istanbul's public baths. It was built in 1474 to provide funds for the mosque and its complex. The dressing room area is huge and covered by impressive domes. It was built as a double bath, and still

serves in that way. The dome over the men's dressing room is bigger, though, than that over the women's area. A pool and sauna have been added to the warm area of the men's side.

Today surrounded by shops, both sections of the Gedikpaşa Bath have rectangular central stones, four washing cubicles, one at each corner and three vaulted ante-chambers. The unique structure of the domes of one of the cubicles is impressive. There are twenty-seven washing basins in the men's side and twenty-one in the women's.

This bath was well known throughout Ottoman history for its many famous "külhanbey." In the hierarchy of all of Istanbul's külhanbeys, those of the Gedikpaşa were traditionally those with the most colorful repute or reputation. (See the chapter on külhanbey in this book for a description of this colorful tradition).

Address	Hamam Cad. No: 65 Gedikpaşa-Eminönü
Telephone	(0 212) 517 89 56
Hours of Operation	05:00-24:00
Price	13 Euros
	Women-Men

Köşk Bath

This bath is located in Cağaloğlu. It used to be known as the Şengül Bath. Quite small because it was originally built as a private bath for the Palace of the Grand Vizier Mahmut Pasha, it was later set aside for use as the public bath of the main shopping district. The exact date of its construction is not known, but it is believed to have been built before Mahmut Pasha's death in 1473.

The plan of the heated section or "sıcaklık" is simple, made up of three bathing cubicles. Today it is, unfortunately, not well maintained, but is open for mixed tourist groups in the evening.

Address	Alayköşkü Cad. No: 17 Cağaloğlu-Eminönü
Telephone	(0 212) 512 73 97
Hours of Operation	08:00-22:00
Price	7 Euros
	Men only but open after 19:00 for mixed groups of tourists.

Vezneciler Bath

This bath is very near the Covered Bazaar, across from the tomb of Kuyucu Murat Pasha. It was commissioned by Grand Vizier Siyavuş Pasha to generate income for the Süleymaniye Complex and is thought to have been built in 1582. The dressing room area was rebuilt using concrete at some time during the centuries after it was originally built, with a resulting loss of much of its historical and architectural integrity. Adjacent to the entrance to the warm area, there is a place for tea to be prepared and the decorations draw one's attention. The bath is generally in an unfortunate state of disrepair.

Address	Bozdoğan Kemeri Cad. No: 2 Vezneciler-Eminönü
Telephone	(0 212) 526 74 58
Hours of Operation	06:00-22:00
Price	10 Euros
	Men Only

Çinili Bath

The Çinili (tiled) Bath in Zeyrek is one of the biggest and most beautiful examples of Ottoman bath architecture. Commissioned by the famous admiral Barbaros Hayrettin Pasha to provide funds for a theological school in Beşiktaş, it was built by Mimar (Architect) Sinan in 1546. The construction of the bath, still used as a double bath as was originally intended, took four years to complete.

The two sections are architecturally identical, with the entrances opening on spacious dressing rooms suffused with beautiful natural light. The domes are 18.5 meters high. There is a beautiful solid marble pool with fountain in the men's section, said to be a gift from the Shah of Iran and added after the restoration done in 1833. Sixteenth century Iznik (Nicaean) tiles were also added later, giving the structure its name, but unfortunately no trace of these remains today.

With original marble basins and railings still in evidence, the heated section of Çinili Bath is classic in form, with an octagonal heated massage platform in the center and cubicles and eyvans forming a square. The doors of the bathing chambers have hexagonal tiles with couplet inscriptions in Persian.

Address	İtfaiye Cad. No: 46 Zeyrek-Fatih
Telephone	(0 212) 631 88 83
Hours of Operation	Women: 10:00-17:00 / Men: 06:30-22:00
Price	14 Euros
	Women-Men

Havuzlu Bath

The Havuzlu Bath is located between Kumkapı and Laleli, next to the site of a square of the same name. There is no information about the date of its construction but it is thought to have been built just after the construction of the Süleymaniye Mosque, finished in 1557. In the small dressing room of Havuzlu Bath is a pool with a fountain. The hot area of the bath is roofed with a large dome. The large main heating octagon stone is situated in the center of this area. A large dome provides space and natural illumination over the central octagon platform. This bath has a very hot sauna. Drawing the attention of the visitor are the small, traditionally Turkish, 'baklava' shaped dome, the Ottoman inscriptions, and the stone bathing basins.

Address	Derinkuyu Sok. No: 16 Nişanca-Eminönü
Telephone	(0 212) 517 54 84
Hours of Operation	07:00-23:00
Price	10 Euros
	Men Only

Nişancı Paşa Bath

The Nişancı Paşa Bath is one of Istanbul's oldest. It was commissioned by the last Grand Vizier of Sultan Fatih, at the same time as the mosque of the same name, in 1475. It was designed as a double bath and continues to be used so. The big, well-lit dressing rooms on the men's side has a pool in the middle; the heated section has three antechambers, four private bathing chambers and an octagonal massage platform. Unfortunately the structure, which has all the characteristics of classic Ottoman architecture, has lost much of its original character.

Address	Türkeli Cad. No: 45 Kumkapı-Eminönü
Telephone	(0 212) 558 09 35
Hours of Operation	Women: 09:00-21:00 / Men: 06:00-23:00
Price	10 Euros
	Women-Men

Kadırga Bath

The Kadırga Bath, in the district called Kadırga just below Sultanahmet, was commissioned in 1506 by the Ottoman governor of the European provinces (Rumeli), Governor General Yahya Pasha, to provide funds for the soup kitchen in Üsküp (Skopje). This bath is still in operation, serving women and men in separate buildings since its construction.

The name of this district, Kadırga, takes its name from the type of warships or galleys that used both sails and oars. These ships were anchored here in the military harbor of Istanbul. The large Kadırga Bath was the place where the Ottoman sailors always took their first baths upon landing. The entrance to the dressing room is under the building that was built right in front of the bath. The large dressing room is covered by a wide and high dome; smaller domes cover the heated section where there is a rectangular central heating stone platform.

Address	Liman Cad. No: 127 Kumkapı-Eminönü
Telephone	(0 212) 518 19 48
Hours of Operation	Women: 10:00-18:00 / Men: 07:00-23:00
Price	12 Euros
	Women-Men

Sofular Bath

The Sofular Bath is located near the Aksaray Metro Station, and is one of the particularly fine public baths of İstanbul, architecturally and otherwise. In the Evliya Çelebi "Book of Travels," it is described as having always been preferred by the "notables" of the city, and still deserves the title of being one of the cleanest, best-maintained and best-managed baths in İstanbul.

It is just across from the Sofular Mosque and was commissioned by Sultan Beyazıt II to generate funds for the mosque complex in Edirne. The date of construction is not known. Designed and still used as a double bath, the sections for men and women are in separate buildings. The dressing room area is covered with a wooden roof and illuminated by a fine roof lantern. The two tiers of changing compartments are clean and well kept. There is also a pool and fountain in the center of this section. The heated section is spacious and light and always very warm, as all Turkish baths should be. In this heated section there are five antechambers, two private bathing cubicles and an octagonal central stone platform in the center of the hot area.

Address	Sofular Cad. No: 66 Aksaray-Fatih
Telephone	(0 212) 521 37 59
Hours of Operation	Women: 8:30-20:00 / Men: 6:00-23:00
Price	10 Euros
	Women-Men

Horhor Bath

The Horhor Bath, and the district it is in, both take their names from the public water fountain that is just behind the bath. Located near the Aksaray Metro Station, this bath was commissioned by Suleyman the Magnificent's Royal Chamberlain Behruz Agha in 1562 as a foundation enterprise designed to generate income for a mosque in another district.

The bath has three tiers of dressing rooms and a heated section covered with a broad dome. There is an octagonal main stone platform in the center, with four private bathing cubicles and three antechambers.

Address	Hamam Sok. No: 8 Aksaray-Fatih
Telephone	(0 212) 521 71 17
Hours of Operation	07:00-23:00
Price	7 Euros
	Men Only

Bostan Bath

The Bostan Bath is near the area of the Haseki Sultan charity complex in Cerrah-
paşa. Thought to have been built during the reign of Sultan Mehmet II, the
Conqueror, its plan is an excellent example of the classic Ottoman bath architecture, laid out in a square, with three antechambers, four private bathing cubicles
and an octagonal main stone platform in the center. Close by the bath is the
tomb of Dellak Dede (Grandfather of washers/scrubbers), who is said to have
bathed the sultan at one time. This double bath is reputed to be one of the
hottest baths in Istanbul.

This very old bath is tucked away among neighboring houses. It has traditionally
been visited for centuries by local women, and they tell many stories about it.
There is an "evliya kurnası," a basin where the women would perform their
ritual ablutions, sometimes leaving a candle as an offering, believing that this
would ensure that offers of marriage for
unmarried girls would soon result. Again in
the women's side, there is a small bathing
cubicle called the şeftali kurnası (peach
basin) where girls who did not want strangers
to see their bodies would bathe. It is said
that Mihrimah Sultan, the daughter of Haseki

Hürrem (Roxelana) and Suleyman the Magnificent always demanded to bathe in private as she had been born with only one breast, and so her mother had the şeftali kurnası arranged for her.

Another legend about the bath is related to a bathing chamber that has been closed up. It is said that the sultan, in disguise, killed (for an unknown reason) the tellak who was washing him, and then had the chamber sealed. Sultan Selim II is also said to have visited the bath in disguise, resulting in the name "hünkar kurnası' (royal basin) being given to the basin/chamber he used. This chamber/basin was set off by beautifully worked iron railings and not used until 1940, when the railings were removed.

Yet another story is that an excellent sweet drink made of tamarind was sold at the door in the years around 1910 by a person named Rüstem Agha. People would come from all over İstanbul just to drink Rüstem Agha's tamarind juice.

Address	Hekimoğlu Ali Paşa Cad. No: 30 Haseki-Fatih
Telephone	(0 212) 586 34 45
Hours of Operation	Women: 8:00-19:00 / Men: 6:30-22:00
Price	7 Euros
	Women-Men

Küçük Bath

The Küçük (small) Bath is just what its name implies: a small bath. Located in Fatih Altımermer, it seems to have been built in 1543. The inscription at the entrance has been partially plastered over and it is thus difficult to read. The dressing room and the heated areas are small; the bath is naturally illuminated with a wooden roof lantern.

Address	Altımermer Cad. No: 1 Şehremini-Fatih
Telephone	(0 212) 585 35 96
Hours of Operation	Women: 9:00-17:00 / Men: 7:00-21:00
Price	7 Euros
	Women-Men

Hacı Kadın Bath

The Hacı Kadın Bath is located on a main thoroughfare called Samatya Hacı Kadın Caddesi, but is not connected in any way with the nearby Hacı Kadın Mosque except in name. The exact date of construction is not known, but a Turkish ambassador to India called Huseyin Efendi commissioned it before he died in 1699, making the construction date sometime around the end of the 17th century. There is a well-lighted dressing room, an intermediate warm area with a pool that was added after the construction, and a heated section of one square area covered by a fairly big dome.

Address	Abdi Çelebi Mah. Hacı Kadın Cad. No: 85 Kocamustafapaşa-Fatih
Telephone	(0 212) 585 93 90
Hours of Operation	Women: 9:30-17:00 / Men: 6:00-9:30 and 17:00-24:00
Price	7 Euros
	Women-Men

Kocamustafapaşa Bath

Kocamustafa Bath is near the mosque of the same name and both of them are in the district of Kocamustafapaşa. The bath was built in 1486. The dome with its wooden roof lantern is over a beautiful dressing room with a pool and fountain in the center. The hot area has a square central stone platform and a sauna. One of the private cubicles is thought to have been used for bathing by Sümbül Efendi, revered by the people as a saint. Above this basin is an original inscription of five lines that can still be seen. There is also a spouting fountain built into an ornamental pool.

The Kocamustafapaşa Bath is one of the public baths of Istanbul that can be recommended as clean and well-maintained.

Address	Kocamustafapaşa Cad. No: 441 Kocamustafapaşa-Fatih
Telephone	(0 212) 529 09 48
Hours of Operation	Women: 8:00-20:00 / Men: 6:00-24:00
Price	7 Euros
	Women-Men

Davutpaşa İskelesi Bath

The Davutpaşa Landing Bath is located opposite the Kasap Ilyas Mosque, which is between the train stations of Yenikapı and Kocamustafapaşa. This is one of the oldest of Istanbul's double baths. The definite date of construction is not known, but it is thought to have been commissioned by the Grand Vizier of Sultan Beyazıt II, Davut Pasha between 1482 and 1498.

This bath is also known as "Zırhcı Bath" or the Armorers' Bath. According to Ottoman tradition, each guild chooses a prophet whose own qualities or trade matched that of the guild and this prophet would be the patron saint or spiritual guide of the guild. Beyazıt II's Grand Vizier shared his name, Davut, with the Prophet Davut (David) the armorer, and that is why the bath is sometimes called "The Armorer."

The bath was extensively modified at the end of the 19th century, changing its general appearance and character. A wooden house was built directly in front of the bath and in 1964 the dressing room of the women's section was converted into a coffeehouse. The hot area has a square plan, and the men's side, very atypically, has two central stone platforms.

Address	Samatya Cad. No: 21 Samatya-Fatih
Telephone	(0 212) 633 22 76
Hours of Operation	Women: 9:30-17:00 / Men: 6:00-23:00
Price	7 Euros
	Women-Men

Hacı Evhadüddin Bath

It is thought that Mimar Sinan built this bath in Yedikule at the same time he built the very nearby mosque of the same name in 1585. The bath was commissioned by the head butcher of the sultan, Hacı Evhadüddin, as a charitable foundation. When first built it is thought to have been a small building which grew larger in time as additions were made. The heated section has a rectangular central stone platform and a fountain with a basin of carved marble.

Address	Hacı Evhadüddin Cad. No: 67 Yedikule-Fatih
Telephone	(0 212) 632 49 24
Hours of Operation	06:00-23:00
Price	7 Euros
	Men Only

Merkez Efendi Bath

This bath is in Topkapı, next to the mosque of the same name. It was commissioned to Architect Sinan by the daughter of Yavuz Sultan Selim, Shah Sultan, in the 16th century. Merkez Efendi, one of the important scholars of the time, is supposed to have bathed in this bath, and there is an abiding superstition that anyone who bathes in the same chamber will be cleansed of any health problem. Until recently, at closing time, a clean towel and wooden clogs would be left in the hot area for the use of Merkez Efendi.

In Ottoman times, the Sünbili sheiks would meet at this bath on the morning of the tenth day of the month of Muharrem of the Muslim calendar to bathe together before going to their lodge and participating in a "aşure" (pudding) ceremony.

Address	Merkez Efendi Mah. Merkez Efendi Cad. No: 5 Zeytinburnu
Telephone	(0 212) 665 44 80
Hours of Operation	06:00-22:00
Price	7 Euros
	Men Only

Mehmet Ağa Bath

First called the Darüssaade Mehmet Ağa Bath, the name has been shortened to Mehmet Ağa Bath. Perhaps the name was changed because this gentleman, who was an administrator of the Ottoman palace, was later executed. In any case, while still in favor and still wealthy enough to commission baths, he had this bath built by the architect, Davut Agha, in 1586. The bath was built in the middle of a residential neighborhood as a double bath with two architecturally similar sections. The bath boasts a spacious and well-illuminated hot section and has an octagonal main stone platform, three private cubicles, and three antechambers.

Address	Beyzeyiz Mah. No: 46 Çarşamba-Fatih
Telephone	(0 212) 521 56 95
Hours of Operation	Women: 9:00-18:00 / Men: 6:00-22:00
Price	7 Euros
	Women-Men

Paşa Bath

Located in the district of Edirnekapı near the Kasım Gönani Mosque, the Paşa Bath (sometimes referred to as the Sultan Bath) is distinct for its small hot area that has managed to retain its original characteristics through the long years since it was first built. The exact date of its construction has not been determined, but we know that it was built at the close of the 15th century by Hatice Sultan, the daughter of Sultan Beyazıt II. The hot area of the Paşa Bath has a small stone platform under a small dome and interconnecting cubicles. Even though it is extremely precious from an historical point of view, this bath is, sadly to say, very poorly maintained today.

Address	Avcıbey Mah. Paşa Hamamı Sok. No: 9 Edirnekapı-Fatih
Telephone	(0 212) 533 73 51
Hours of Operation	07:00-22:00
Price	7 Euros
	Men Only

Arabacılar Bath

The Arabacılar Bath (bath for carriage drivers) is in the district of Ayvansaray along the Golden Horn. It is believed that the bath was built during the period of the Ottoman conquest of Istanbul (1453). The bath has rounded arches, resembling a Byzantine structure. The current bath was built over the original structure and the "new" building dates to the beginning of the 18th century.

This single bath was later changed to provide a women's section, this alteration serving to destroy much of the original features of the building. While there is a space for the inscriptions, the area is bare today giving us no clues as to construction date or other information. Unlike the classical Ottoman bath, this bath receives very little natural light.

Arabacılar Bath got its name from the fact that the neighborhood in which it stands was traditionally a gypsy neighborhood and that, at that time, many Istanbul gypsies worked as carriage drivers. The mosque is called the Yataghan Mosque and so sometimes the bath is also called by this name. The bath today is in a poor state of maintenance.

Address	Yatağan Hamam Sok. No: 1 Balat-Fatih
Telephone	(0 212) 525 07 35
Hours of Operation	06:00-21:00
Price	7 Euros
	Women-Men

Çavuş Bath

The Balat Çavuş Bath is directly adjacent to the Ferruh Kethüda Mosque, itself a work of the master architect, Mimar Sinan. One of the city's oldest baths, there is no document existing that clearly states when and by whom the bath was commissioned and built. It is believed, though, that this bath dates to the time of the conquest (mid 15th century) or from the time of Beyazıt II (late 15th century). A charitable foundation document dating from the time of the conquest speaks of two baths in the Balat neighborhood, and researchers believe that this might be one of these baths mentioned. Similar to the fate of many of the historic baths of Istanbul, the dressing room area of the Balat Çavuş Bath was completely altered over the centuries. The bath was traditionally used by Jewish Ottomans and had a pool that does not exist today. Today this ancient bath is in a state of disrepair, both in terms of its architectural integrity and its management.

Address	Çavuş Hamam Sok. No: 11 Balat-Fatih
Telephone	(0 212) 521 66 64
Hours of Operation	Women: 09:00-18:00 / Men: 07:00-23:00
Price	7 Euros
	Women-Men

Tahta Minare Bath

The Tahta Minare Bath, built as a means to finance and maintain the Sadrazam Koca Ragip Pasha Library, is located along the Golden Horn in Balat, a UNESCO historical preservation area, and stands adjacent to the mosque of the same name. Since the Sadrazam died in 1763, the bath must have been built shortly after his death. The two-tiered dressing room area is illuminated by a roof lantern with ten windows.

Walking towards the warm area of the bath, one passes by a beautifully worked marble fountain, today used as a tea station. The hot section of the bath has four cubicles at its corners and three antechambers between.

Address	Vodina Cad. No: 95 Balat-Fatih
Telephone	(0 212) 525 24 45
Hours of Operation	Women: Mondays through Thursdays 11:00-17:00;
	Men: Mondays through Thursdays 6:00-11:00/17:00-23:00
	Other days: 6:00-23:00
Price	7 Euros
	Women-Men

Park Bath

The Park Bath is referred to as the Acı or "Bitter" Bath in old records. This bath is located in the street across from Firuz Ağa Mosque near Sultanahmet Square.

A single bath, there is no definite date as to when it was built or by whom, but it is known to have been built for the purpose of providing revenue for the Fenari İsa Mosque, and to have been commissioned by Molla Fenarizade Alaeddin Ali Efendi, an academic of the Fatih period. From this we can deduce that it was probably built around the end of the 15th century. It is mentioned in the map of Istanbul waterways produced at the end of the 16th century. At this time, the bath got its water from the same source as the nearby Topkapı Palace.

Address	Divanyolu Cad. No: 10 Sultanahmet-Eminönü
Telephone	(0 212) 513 72 04
Hours of Operation	07:00-22:00
Price	10 Euros
	Men Only

Küçükpazar Bath

The Küçükpazar Bath is in the district of the same name, located between Unkapanı and Eminönü. It was commissioned as a single bath for the purpose of generating income for the soup kitchen of Rum (Greek-speaking Ottoman citizen) Mehmet Pasha. The exact date of its construction is not known, but it is known that Rum Mehmet Pasha was discharged from office and executed in 1469, so the Küçükpazar Bath must be one of the oldest public baths in İstanbul. The dressing room area of this well-illuminated bath has been, unfortunately, modified. The hot area has a rectangular central stone platform.

Address	Hacı Kadın Cad. No: 134 Küçükpazar-Eminönü
Telephone	(0 212) 526 37 95
Hours of Operation	06:00-21:00
Price	10 Euros
	Men Only

Galatasaray Bath

Managed by the same person since 1956, the Galatasaray Bath is the best-maintained and the most beautiful bath in all of Beyoğlu. The bath is just off İstiklal Caddesi on the short street that runs alongside the wall of the famous Galatasaray Lycée.

The Galatasaray Bath was built in 1715 directly adjacent to the school that was later to become the Francophone, Galatasaray Lycée. Built as a single-style public bath, the bath was primarily used for many long years by the school's boarding students and the bath was closed to the public during the morning hours while the students were bathing. The bath underwent major restoration work in 1965. At that time a women's section was also added to the structure. The men's dressing room area (an original feature) is very clean, functional, and exquisitely beautiful. Passing through the warm area, the bather enters a classical, square-plan hot bathing area with the central stone platform at its very center. The hot area has four cubicles at the corners and three antechambers between.

The "pasha" cubicle is very eye-catching. While not an original feature, the red marble stripes built into the walls add even more beauty to the setting.

Traditionally, the Galatasaray Bath was a destination point for male revelers of the rather elite set who needed a place to rest after a night of drinking in the Bohemian districts of Beyoğlu. Those who had also done a lot of drinking but didn't have the financial wherewithal to spend what was left of the night at the Galatasaray would walk down the hill to less posh Ağa Bath.

The Galatasaray Bath is one of the few baths in Istanbul that we can recommend fully without hesitation. This bath is a favorite drawing card for tourists and the bath will allow mixed groups of twenty or more.

Address	İstiklal Cad. Turnacıbaşı Sok. No: 24 Beyoğlu
Telephone	(0 212) 252 42 42
Hours of Operation	Men 6:00-22:00 / Women 8:00-20:00
Price	30 Euros
	Women-Men / Mixed groups

Kılıç Ali Paşa Bath

The Ottoman Admiral of the Fleet, Kılıç Ali Pasha, commissioned the building of the Kılıç Ali Paşa Bath and its adjacent mosque. Its construction date is unknown but the bath was built by Sinan shortly before the mosque that dates to 1583.

Today the bath cries out for repair, but even in its poor state it still reflects the grandeur of masterpiece architecture and bears Sinan's stamp with its large, light, and magnificent dome. This bath has a feature that is very original as it has two doors leading from the dressing room area to the warm area. The hot area is roofed by a large dome that provides a great deal of natural light. There are three cubicles and six antechambers in this section. The Kılıç Ali Paşa Bath was built as a single bath and continues to function in this way.

Address	Medrese Sok. No: 24 Tophane-Beyoğlu
Telephone	(0 212) 293 70 37
Hours of Operation	06:00-24:00
Price	10 Euros
	Men Only

Ağa Bath

Jutting to the east off of Beyoğlu's main street of İstiklal, we walk down the hill to Çukurcuma, a section of the city that is in early stages of gentrification. The bath was built in 1562 by Yakup Agha, the head white Eunuch of the palace, to provide operational funds for the Fenerbahçe Lighthouse.

Through its almost 500 years of operations, the bath has seen numerous modifcations. Today the bath has a three-tier dressing room. Although this area was most likely built of wood, in the early 20th century the wood was replaced by a stone-brick construction. Located here is a beautiful fountain with an ornamental pool. The bath's hot area still reflects some of the bath's original features; it is built in the classical square plan and has three antechambers.

The Agha has the interesting feature of being one of Istanbul's traditional 24-

hour baths, a place where revelers can spend at least a few hours sleeping after a long night on the town in Beyoğlu. This was/is an ideal place for those who either were too drunk to go home, or who didn't want to go home. The few hours of sleep are followed by a bath that puts the body back into action so the party-goer can face a new day without a hangover. The Agha still continues with this tradition.

Address	Turnacıbaşı Sok. No: 60 Beyoğlu
Telephone	(0 212) 249 50 27
Hours of Operation	Women: every day 7:00-18:00, but closed on Sundays / Men: All day on Sundays and, on other days, all hours except for the hours that the bath is open to women.
Price	10 Euros
	Women-Men

Firuz Ağa Bath

Also known as the Çukurcuma Bostanbaşı Bath, the Firuz Ağa Bath is situated between the two districts of Beyoğlu and Tophane. Its exact construction date has not been fixed, but it is believed to have been built after 1831. Built as a single bath, today it provides services to both men and women, but at different hours of the day.

Address	Çukurcuma Cad. No: 6 Beyoğlu
Telephone	(0 212) 244 58 50
Hours of Operation	Women: Every day 10:00-17:00, but closed on Sundays. Men: All day Sunday and from 6:00-10:00 and17:00-24:00 on other days.
Price	10 Euros
	Women-Men

Çukurcuma Süreyya Bath

The Çukurcuma Bath of Galatasaray is directly opposite the Muhiddin Molla Fenari Mosque. No one is exactly sure when the bath was built but we do know that in 1831 Nakşidil Sultan was responsible for locating major water supplies for Beyoğlu, so it is supposed that this bath must have been built after this.

The dressing room section of the bath has been completely remodeled, so the bath does not retain any of its original features. The hot area of the bath consists of 12 washing stations placed around a square central stone platform.

Address	Çukurcuma Cad. No: 57 Tophane-Beyoğlu
Hours of Operation	09:00-21:00
Price	10 Euros
	Men Only

Büyük Bath

Büyük means "large," and this is an apt name for this huge bath that is situated next to the Kasımpaşa Mosque. Not only is this a large bath but it is also one of Istanbul's cleanest and hottest bathing establishments. The bath was commissioned by Güzelce Kasım Pasha, the personage who gave the district his name. Both the bath and its adjacent mosque were built in 1533 by Sinan. It still functions as a double bath.

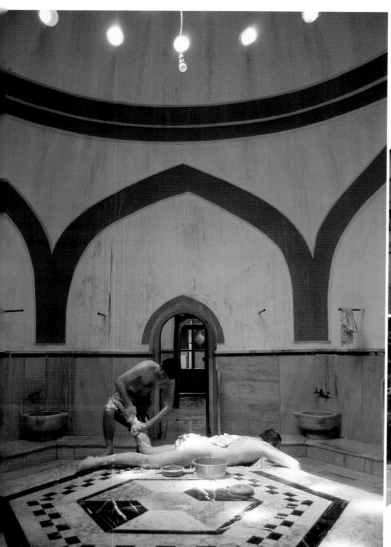

Both sides of the bath have spacious and beautifully illuminated dressing rooms. A large, modern, swimming/bathing pool was added later to the men's section. In summer months the pool can be entered independently with payment of a separate fee. The men's hot area of the Büyük Bath consists of six cubicles that fan out around

the hexagonal central stone platform. The hot area, with its sauna, is roofed by large domes. In every detail that captures our eyes, the bath seems to shout that it was built by the Ottoman's master architect and builder. Another surprising feature is that the hot area is so large that it includes a total of sixty washing stations. The Büyük Bath has the advantage of being Istanbul's largest working bath.

Address	Potinciler Sok. No: 22 Kasımpaşa-Beyoğlu
Telephone	(0 212) 253 42 29
Hours of Operation	Women: 08:00-19:00 / Men: 06:00-23:00
Price	10 Euros
	Women-Men

Hürriyet Bath

The Hürriyet (Freedom) Bath in Istanbul's district of Dolapdere is also known as the Anayasa (Constitution) Bath. The bath was built in 1911, immediately subsequent to the enactment of constitutional freedom in Turkey, and that is why it bears these names as the Ottoman witness to a long battle for popular freedom. The front façade of the bath has inscriptions of "Constitution Bath" written in Armenian and Greek, with a Turkish inscription, 'Yenişehir Hürriyet Bath.'

The bath is a single type bath with washing stations but no private cubicles. The hot section of the bath is roofed with a large dome. This bath is the "newest" of the historic baths of Turkey, and unlike its older counterparts was built as a privately owned venture.

Address	Gölbaşı Sok. No: 80 Dolapdere-Beyoğlu
Telephone	(0 212) 254 32 32
Hours of Operation	06:00-24:00
Price	7 Euros
	Men Only

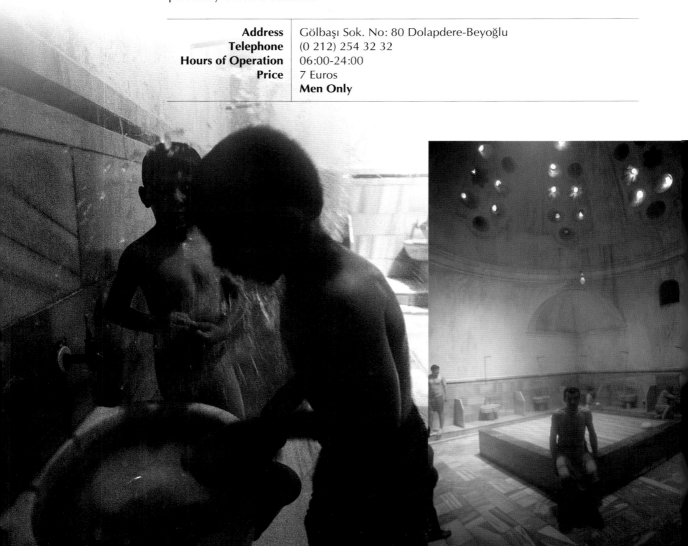

Sarıyer Bath

Located at the northern end of the European side of the Bosphorus Strait, the Sarıyer Bath was built to provide operating funds for the Zekeriyaköy Mosque. Its date of construction is not known but it is believed to have been built somewhere during the early years of the 17th century. The hot area of the bath has five cubicles, two antechambers, and a square central stone platform.

Address	Yenimahalle Cad. No: 65 Sarıyer
Telephone	(0 212) 271 03 20
Hours of Operation	Women: 09:00-19:00 / Men: 06:30-23:00
Price	7 Euros
	Women-Men

Beşiktaş Bath

Until very recently the Beşiktaş Bath in the district that bears its name was known as the Köyiçi (village center) Bath. There is no written record of its construction, leading us to believe that since it is not listed on any of the foundation ledgers, it must have been built as a private enterprise. The bath has been repaired frequently during the past century. Today it ranks as a clean, neighborhood type bath.

Address	Ihlamurdere Cad. Şair Veysi Sok. No: 12 Beşiktaş
Telephone	(0 212) 261 03 77
Hours of Operation	Women: 08:00-19:30 / Men: 06:00-23:00
Price	10 Euros
	Women-Men

İstinye Bath

The İstinye Bath is one of the very few baths located along the Bosphorus. This bath is in the village of İstinye and is opposite the Neslişah Hanım Sultan Mosque. Since the bath was commissioned by Gazi Ali Pasha, one of the Ottoman pashas who participated in the siege and conquest of Istanbul, it is believed to have been built soon after the 1453 conquest, making it one of the oldest Ottoman baths in the city.

The bath was built as a double bath, but the women's section of the bath was torn down many, many years ago. Today the men's warm area has a sauna. The Istinye bath is small, clean, and well-maintained. The bath has a parking lot for easy access.

Address	Değirmen Sok. No: 35 İstinye-Sarıyer
Telephone	(0 212) 277 52 04
Hours of Operation	06:00-23:00
Price	10 Euros
	Men Only

Çinili Bath

There are two baths in Istanbul that are termed "çinili" or "tiled." The tiled bath of Üsküdar was commissioned in 1648 by Kösem Sultan and built by the architect, Kasım Agha, as part of the Çinili charity complex. Unfortunately, today the bath is "tiled" only in name, for none of its original tiles are still extant.

The bath is the largest building in the complex and is opposite the Çinili Mosque. It was built as a double bath and continues to operate as such. The two sides are not the same, as the women's side of the bath is larger than the men's. The square dressing room area is roofed with a number of domes. The men's dressing room has a fountain and ornamental pool. The warm areas are rectangular in shape and are roofed by domes, four over the women's side and three over the men's. Rather atypically for Turkish baths, both men's and women's sections of the Çinili Bath are quite different. The women's is built in an octagonal plan, while the men's side in square and, keeping in line with classical Ottoman bath architecture, is supported by three antechambers.

By the beginning of the 20th century the Çinili Bath was in such a bad state of disrepair that it lay abandoned until, in 1964, it passed into private hands. The new owners restored the building and reopened it for use. Today the men's section has a sauna. The Çinili Bath is one of Istanbul's cleanest and best-maintained baths and is among those that we can fully recommend.

Address	Çavuşdere Cad. No: 204 Üsküdar
Telephone	(0 216) 333 15 93
Hours of Operation	Women: 08:00-18:30 / Men: 05:30-23:00
Price	12 Euros
	Women-Men

Valide Atik Bath

The Valide Atik Bath of Üsküdar is located in the Toptaşı (cannonball) neighborhood so it is also often referred to as the Toptaşı. The bath was built by Sinan in 1583 as part of the Valide Atik Charity Complex. Originally the dressing room area had a wooden roof but in the recent past this was replaced by a concrete roof. The dressing rooms in this area are clean and well-maintained. Similar to almost all Sinan baths, this structure too has a square-plan hot area with four cubicles and three antechambers.

The Valide Atik Bath is clean and well-maintained and among those that we recommend.

Address	Eski Toptaşı Cad. No: 104 Üsküdar
Telephone	(0 216) 334 91 58
Hours of Operation	Women: 08:00-19:00 / Men: 06:00-23:00
Price	10 Euros
	Women-Men

Ağa Bath

Just a short walk away from the Üsküdar Square, the Ağa Bath was commissioned by Malatayalı Ismail Agha, Sultan Ahmed I's Keeper of the Pantry. The bath is part of a complex composed of mosque and dervish lodge that were built in 1610. The Ağa Bath was built as a double bath and still functions as such. The Ağa Bath closely resembles a traditional Ottoman house with its long bay window stretching between floors. The wooden dressing room area of the men's section receives a great deal of natural light through the large, octagonal roof lantern. The hot section repeats the plan with an octagonal central stone platform surrounded by private cubicles and three antechambers. This small neighborhood bath is both clean and attractive.

Address	Gündoğumu Cad. No: 65 Üsküdar
Telephone	(0 216) 333 38 27
Hours of Operation	Women: 08:00-18:30 / Men: 06:00-23:00
Price	10 Euros
	Women-Men

Şifa Bath

Until the 1960s the Şifa (good health) Bath located in central Üsküdar was known as the Eski (old) Bath, due to the fact that this is the oldest bath of Üsküdar. Some sources refer to it as the Rum (Greek) Mehmed Paşa Bath. The date of its construction has not been fixed, but it is believed to have been built in the late 15th century. The bath was built as a double bath. Surprisingly, for a structure this old, the bath has managed to cling to much of its original features and continues to function as a double bath. Quite different from the traditional Turkish bath, though, both men's and women's sections are entered from the same street. The two sections of the bath are adjacent to each other and mirror each other architecturally. The Şifa Bath is built on the classic cross style with an octagonal central stone platform surrounded by four antechambers and four cubicles with two basins each.

Address	Doğancılar Cad. No: 54 Üsküdar
Telephone	(0 216) 333 27 87
Hours of Operation	Women: 09:00-17:00 / Men: 06:00-21:00
Price	10 Euros
	Women-Men

Bulgurlu Bath

The Bulgurlu Bath of Üsküdar is located near the neighborhood mosque. This small bath was built in 1618 by Aziz Mahmut Hüdayi Efendi, the founder of the Celveti sect and the imam chosen to give the first sermon at the opening of the Sultanahmet (Blue) Mosque in 1616. This event is documented by the still intact inscription on the wall of the dressing room area. The tiny bath still carefully maintains the basin from which Aziz Mahmut Hüdayi Efendi washed. Until the first quarter of the 20th century candles over the basin were lit in the evenings. Many still hold that the water from this basin has curative powers.

Address	Bulgurlu Cad. No: 47 Üsküdar
Telephone	(0 216) 481 00 70
Hours of Operation	Women: Wednesday 10:00-17:00 / Men: Wednesdays 6:00-10:00 and 17:00-23:00, other days 6:00-23:00
Price	7 Euros
	Women-Men

Aziziye Bath

The Aziziye Bath is one of the two historic baths of Kadıköy that are still operational. Located near the ferry docks, the bath was built during the reign of Sultan Abdülaziz (1861-1876) and took its name from the Sultan's second name. There is no documentation, however, as to when it was built or who commissioned it or for what purpose.

The bath still functions as a double bath, as it was when first built. Built in the center of Kadıköy (ancient Chalcedon), the Azizye Bath is clean and has efficient management. It's one of those we recommend.

Address	Rıhtım Cad. Recaizade Sok. No: 19 Kadıköy
Telephone	(0 216) 349 14 65
Hours of Operation	Women: 08:00-19:00 / Men: 06:00-23:00
Price	10 Euros
	Women-Men

Çarşı Bath

The Çarşı (market) Bath stands near the Kadıköy ferryboat docks. This very old bath was built by Fazıl Efendi as a means to raise money to maintain the Yeniköy Mosque. No one knows its exact construction date but Fazıl Efendi died in 1583 so it has to be earlier than that date. Today the bath is dwarfed by the shops that surround it on all sides. The Çarşı Bath has a beautiful marble fountain in its dressing room area. The Çarşı Bath has been radically changed over the years and retains little of its original architectural details. A number of later additions were also tacked onto the building.

Address	Söğütlüçeşme Cad. No: 34 Kadıköy
Telephone	(0 216) 338 10 05
Hours of Operation	06:00-23:00
Price	10 Euros
	Men Only

Beykoz Bath

The Beykoz Bath is located on the road that runs from the Bosphorus waterfront to the Beykoz Square, in the vicinity of the On Parmak (ten finger) Fountain. The bath was built by Suleyman the Great's Royal Chamberlain, Behruz Agha, as part of a charitable foundation. We know that Behruz Agha had a mosque built in 1562 so we assume that the bath, too, must date from around this general time. According to some documents the bath was a work of Mimar Sinan, but there are also other claims to the contrary. The bath is among a very small handful of old buildings in Beykoz. Although it was originally built as a double bath, today the Beykoz bath operates as a single/shared bath.

Address	Fevzipaşa Cad. No: 14 Beykoz
Telephone	(0 216) 323 92 66
Hours of Operation	Women: Mondays 10:00-17:00 / Men: Mondays 5:00-10:00 and 17:00-24:00, all other days 5:00-24:00
Price	7 Euros
	Women-Men

Beylerbeyi Bath

In close proximity to the Beylerbeyi ferry docks, the Beylerbeyi Bath is part of a large charitable complex consisting of the bath, a mosque, a primary school and two water fountains built by Sultan Abdülhamit I in 1789. The bath with its square dressing room area is fronted on the street side by a house that was a later addition. This same section also has a fountain with a broad basin, an old mirror with a wooden frame and a clock that is also a valuable antique. The rectangular hot area has a square central stone platform. The bath boasts two original stone basins that display beautiful verbiage stone work. The bath operates as a bath shared by men and women.

Address	Yalıboyu Cad. No: 70 Beylerbeyi-Üsküdar
Telephone	(0 216) 321 46 83
Hours of Operation	Women: Mondays, Tuesday, Thursday, Saturday 10:00-17:00
	Men: Monday, Tuesday, Thursday, Saturday 5:30-10:00
	and 17:00-24:00; Wednesday, Friday, Sunday 5:30-24:00
Price	7 Euros
	Women-Men

Yalı Bath

The Yalı Bath is located in the district of Maltepe and is in the neighborhood of the Feyzullah Efendi Mosque. It is believed that the bath was commissioned by Yusuf Agha, the assistant to the Grand Vizier, and built in the years 1771-1773 as a foundation to support a school also built in the Cağaloğlu neighborhood. The small and very plain Yalı Bath is devoid of any outstanding architectural features. The stone basin in the dressing room area is worth a look, though.

Address	Yalı Mah. Hamam Sok. No: 4 Maltepe
Telephone	(0 216) 305 80 31
Hours of Operation	Women: 08:00-19:00 / Men: 06:00-24:00
Price	7 Euros
	Women-Men

Şifa Bath

Kartal is a district that is at the very farthest reaches of old Istanbul. Today this old bath is surrounded on three sides by huge work and business centers, seemingly dwarfed among these disparate structures. The Şıfa (good health) Bath was commissioned as a single bath by Hadji Mustafa Pasha in 1807. Still operating, the bath today is, unfortunately, in a very poorly maintained state.

Address	Hürriyet Caddesi No: 3/A Kartal
Telephone	(0 216) 353 50 07
Hours of Operation	07:00-23:00
Price	7 Euros
	Men Only

Yakacık Bath

Even today the neighborhood of Yakacık in the district of Kartal remains an out-of-the-way place, both in terms of distance to the city center and in population density. No sources can be found that give us any information about this old neighborhood bath. We do know that the oldest bath in the area was built by Dervish Ali Efendi who died in 1709 and so it is believed that the bath is contemporary. Although closed for many years and only recently reopened, the bath is very poorly maintained.

Address	Çarşı Mah. Vezirçeşme Sok. No: 4 Yakacık-Kartal
Telephone	(0 216) 451 52 87
Hours of Operation	08:00-23:00
Price	10 Euros
	Men Only

References

- İstanbul Hamamları , M. Nermi Haskan, TURİNG Yayını, 1995
- Türk Hamamları Etüdü, Kemal Ahmet Aru, Thesis for the Associate Professorship, İTÜ Mimarlık Fakültesi Yayını, 1941
- Anadolu'da 12. ve 13. Yüzyıl Türk Hamamları, Prof. Dr. M. Yılmaz Önge, Vakıflar Genel Müdürlüğü Yayınları
- İznik Büyük Hamam ve Osmanlı Devri Hamamları Hakkında Bir Deneme, Prof. Dr. Semavi Eyice, Tarih Dergisi 12. Sayı, Eylül 1960
- Yabancı Seyyahların Gözüyle 16. Yüzyıl İstanbul'unda Hamamlar ve Temizlik, Prof. Dr. Metin And, Gündelik Hayatın Renkleri-İstanbul Armağanı, 3. Cilt içinde, İstanbul Büyükşehir Belediyesi Yayınları
- Türk Hamamının Kültürümüzde ve Sanatımızda Yeri, Metin And, Ulusal Kültür Dergisi, Sayı 5, Temmuz 1979
- İstanbul Hamamları, Şinasi Akbatu, 1973 İstanbul İl Yıllığı
- Kadın Hamamları, Ercüment Ekrem Talu, Türk Yazarlarının Kaleminden Bir Hayal İstanbul içinde, derleyen Necati Güngör, Milliyet Yayınları, 1997
- İstanbul 7 Tepe Hamamlarına Dair Bazı Notlar, Vakıflar Dergisi, A. Süheyl Ünver, sayı 2, 1942
- Türk Hamamı, A. Süheyl Ünver, Türk Tarih Kurumu Basımevi, 1973
- 1147 (1734) tarihli Hamamcı Defteri, M. Cevdet Yaz, Atatürk Kitaplığı, No: B.6
- Bergama'da Hamamlar, Bugünkü Hamamlar, Küplü Hamam, Parasız Hamam, Hamam Eğlenceleri, Osman Bayatlı, Fikirler Dergisi, Sayı 7, 1943
- İstanbul'un Taşı Toprağa Altın, Sennur Sezer-Adnan Özyalçıner, Altın Kitaplar
- Osmanlı'da Seks Sarayda Gece Dersleri, Murat Bardakçı, Gür Yayınları, 1994
- Türkiye Tarihi-Osmanlı Devletine Kadar Türkler, Halil Berktay, Ümit Hassan, Ayla Ödekan, Cilt 1, Cem Yayınevi, 1997
- İstanbul Mektupları, Basiretçi Ali Efendi, Kitabevi
- Eski Zamanlarda İstanbul Hayatı, Balıkhane Nazırı, A. Rıza Bey, Kitabevi, 2001
- İstanbul Gizemleri: Büyüler, Yatırlar, İnançlar, Giovanni Scognamillo, Altın Kitaplar, 1993
- Eski İstanbul'da Gündelik Hayat, İ. Gündağ – Ersu Pelin, İstanbul Büyükşehir Belediyesi Yayınları
- Osmanlı Adet Merasim ve Tabirleri, Abdülaziz Bey, Tarih Vakfı Yurt Yayınları
- Baron Vratislav'ın Anıları, Milliyet Yayınları, 1998
- 18. Asırda İstanbul, P.G. İncician, 1976
- Eski İstanbul Yaşayışı, Musahipzade Celal, 1947-1992
- İstanbul Hatıratı, Panaroma, 2 cilt, 1911
- Asırlar Boyunca İstanbul, Haluk Şehsuvaroğlu
- İstanbul Argosu ve Halk Tabirleri, Mehmet Halit Bayrı, 1934
- Geçen Yüzyılda İstanbul'da Kabadayılar ve Külhanbeyleri, Server Tanilli, Osmanlı İmparatorluğu'nda Yaşamak içinde, İletişim, 2000
- Kabadayı, Külhanbeyi ve Mahalle Tosunları, R.C. Ulunay, İstanbul İçin Şehrengiz içinde, 1991
- İstanbul Hamamları, Kamuran Günel, Lisans Tezi, 1959, İÜ Edebiyat Fakültesi Sanat Tarihi Bölümü
- Mimar Sinan'ın İstanbul'daki Mevcut Hamamları, Mimar Ali Dost Ertuğrul, Yüksek Lisans Tezi, İTÜ Fen Bilimleri Enstitüsü, 2002
- İstanbul Ansiklopedisi, Reşat Ekrem Koçu, 1958
- Dünden Bugüne İstanbul Ansiklopedisi, Kültür Bakanlığı-Tarih Vakfı ortak yayını, 1994
- Tanzimat'tan Cumhuriyete Türkiye Ansiklopedisi, İletişim Yayınları, 1985
- Türkiye Diyanet Vakfı İslam Ansiklopedisi, 1988
- Milli Eğitim Bakanlığı İslam Ansiklopedisi, 1950
- Türkçe'nin Büyük Argo Sözlüğü, Hulki Aktunç, YKY Yayınları, 1998